THE LANGUAGE OF A WORK OF ART

THE PRINCIPLES OF APPRECIATION AND CREATION OF WORKS OF ART

BY

NORMAN B. GULAMERIAN

LIONIZE, INC.

SECOND EDITION

LIONIZE, INC.
New York, New York

First Edition Originally Published in 1963 by The Art and Art Education Studies Division, Utrecht Linens, Inc.

Library of Congress Control Number: 2001091638

Printed in the United States of America

For quantity purchases, contact Utrecht Art Supplies, School Services Division,
6 Corporate Drive, Cranbury NJ 08512 Toll Free: 800-223-9132
Info at UtrechtArt.com or order online at www.UtrechtArt.com

Cover: Claude Monet's THE FOUR TREES. Oil on canvas, 1891. The Metropolitan Museum of Art,
H.O. Havemeyer Collection, Bequest of Mrs. H.O. Havemeyer, 1929
(29.100.110) Photograph © 1996 The Metropolitan Museum of Art

Cover design by Ariel Delacroix
Text design by Sandra Leigh Baker

TO MY PARENTS
- NBG

ACKNOWLEDGEMENTS

I wish to express my gratitude to Mary Doherty and Rebecca Akhan at the Metropolitan Museum of Art, Stacy Bomento at the Philadelphia Museum of Art, Carmen Sanchez at Museo Nacional Centro de Arte Reina Sofia, Tom Lisanti at the New York Public Library, Nancy Boyle Press at the Baltimore Museum of Art, Crystal Gauen at the Museum of Modern Art and Meglena Zapreva-Kirkbride and Kate Gerlough at the Frick Museum for their assistance in supplying photographs of the works of art in their collections and for granting permission to reproduce them in this book.

I would also like to thank the following for their enthusiasm, help and guidance: Sandra Leigh Baker, Olivia Blumer, Barbara Bowen, Leonard Charney, Diane Dax, Tricia DeFelice, Michael Montana and Wahid Maqsudi. And to Jim Peters and Mike Gundry at Utrecht for recognizing the value and importance of making this book available to a whole new generation of artists.

June 2001

The Publisher
LIONIZE, INC.

CONTENTS

PREFACE TO THE *SECOND EDITION*

One of the major aims of this course, through the combination of the text and exercises is to lead to the stimulation and to contribute to the development of the student's potential artistic abilities. Artistic abilities basically involve the understanding of the language of a work of art, the ability to analyze and appreciate, the ability to produce creative visual and expressive ideas, the ability to organize them into a work of art, and the ability to make aesthetic judgments.

The plan of the course is to make a concrete and systematic presentation of all the important principles and factors in the appreciation and creation of works of art. Every factor and principle discussed in this course is demonstrated with examples of works of art and/or with the aid of diagrams.

This information is further reinforced with a carefully planned sequence of exercises by which it is hoped the student will gain a deeper insight into the world of art. Also accompanying the text is a set of pre-outlined exercises which eliminates the tedious task of the student rendering identical line drawings necessary for the special exercises.

I've made a few changes and additions to the text.

Also, since the publication of the first edition of THE LANGUAGE Of A WORK OF ART, I've written several articles for publication in the 60s and 70s. These articles were based in part on the 1965 paper "An Objective Theory on the Assessment of Artistic Production" which I read at the 73rd Annual American Psychological Association National Convention at the invitation of Harry Helson, then president of the Division of Aesthetics.

Rudolf Arnheim read "An Objective Theory on the Assessment of Artistic Production" and made helpful comments, from which I benefited when writing the final draft. I also wish to express my thanks to Rudolf Arnheim for the many conversations we had in the past on problems of art, which contributed toward the shaping of my thinking over the years.

In the first part of "Objective Theory of the Assessment of Artistic Production" I attempted to develop an approach to classify the basic "whole qualities" and/or structural devices which are to describe and aid in the production of visual concepts of cradled and uncradled order which can have different degrees of ordered complexity, concepts which were integrated into those articles.

The diagrams which appear in the book were drawn by my brother Harold E. Gulamerian.

APRIL 2001

NBG

The Visual Elements of a Work of Art

The three basic visual elements of a work of art are shape, brightness and color. These are the building blocks with which the artists creates order in the work of art in the picture plane. The picture plane is the flat, two-dimensional surface on which the artist works, such as paper or canvas. The correct understanding of the individual characteristics of the three visual elements is essential. In this section only, the basic elements of shape, color and brightness are treated individually for the purpose of defining them clearly. However, in the following sections we will emphasize the importance of these three building blocks of art by describing how they function together to help determine the even more important visual characteristics of structure and expression of the work of art.

The Nature and Character of Shape

Shape is a fundamental factor in every work of art because color and brightness can not exist without shape. The artist uses shape to create the order which is particular to a work of art. The knowledge of the major properties of shape can greatly aid our understanding and the creation of works of art. The concepts of shape and form have been carefully investigated by Rudolf Arnheim in the classic work, *Art and Visual Perception*, 1959.

The Major Properties of Visual Shape

A. *Boundary:* Boundary may be defined as a coherent or almost coherent outline which can be made up, for example, of lines or points. The boundary encloses or makes distinct a given visual area.

B. *Structural Axis*: The structural axis or axes are the dominant directional and structural aspects of the visual shape. Structural axes are often strongly dependent upon the boundary of the shape. The structural axes can have a variety of characteristics, i.e., straight or curved. The same major structural axes may derive from different boundaries. For example, the major structural axes of both the Empire State Building and a tall pine tree are strong verticals. However, the boundaries of the shape of the building and the tree are entirely different. The boundary is dynamic in that it actively serves to separate the enclosed area from its surroundings. The dynamic aspect of the structural axes may be described as the sense of direction they instill within the shape. These two forces together, the axes and the boundaries, determine the general characteristics of the shape. By simply drawing a variety of shapes and carefully indicating their structural axes (that is the dominant directional characteristics) the artist and student can greatly contribute to his understanding and knowledge of the two factors that determine shape (*Figure 1*).

We have reproduced a drawing (*Figure 2*) of "St. Christopher" by Giovanni Antonio de Pordenone (1484 - 1539). The work is squared so the artist can copy the drawing to another surface. We see in addition to the usual horizontal square drawn with red chalk, it has also been squared in a diagonal direction in black chalk. This diagonal square repeats the major diagonal axes of the form of St. Christopher. The artist no doubt found it more natural and easier to copy the drawing of St. Christopher in following the major axes of the form.

C. *The Nature of Points and Lines*: A pure line is one that does not enclose a certain area. An example of this would be a straight line or a slightly arched line that does not outline or enclose a specific, clear-cut area. A pure line is identical with its structural axis.

One might object that a wavy line, such as shown (*Figure 3*), has its structural axis drawn down the center, and that therefore in this case the structural axis of a line is not identical with the line itself. This, however, happens only when a line begins to enclose an area. This involves the factor of closure which will be discussed further on.

A single fine point placed on a homogeneous or flat surface by itself without a clear reference to the borders of the picture plane is visually unstable and ambiguous. It does not possess a definite direction, as does a shape containing a structural axis. However, although a

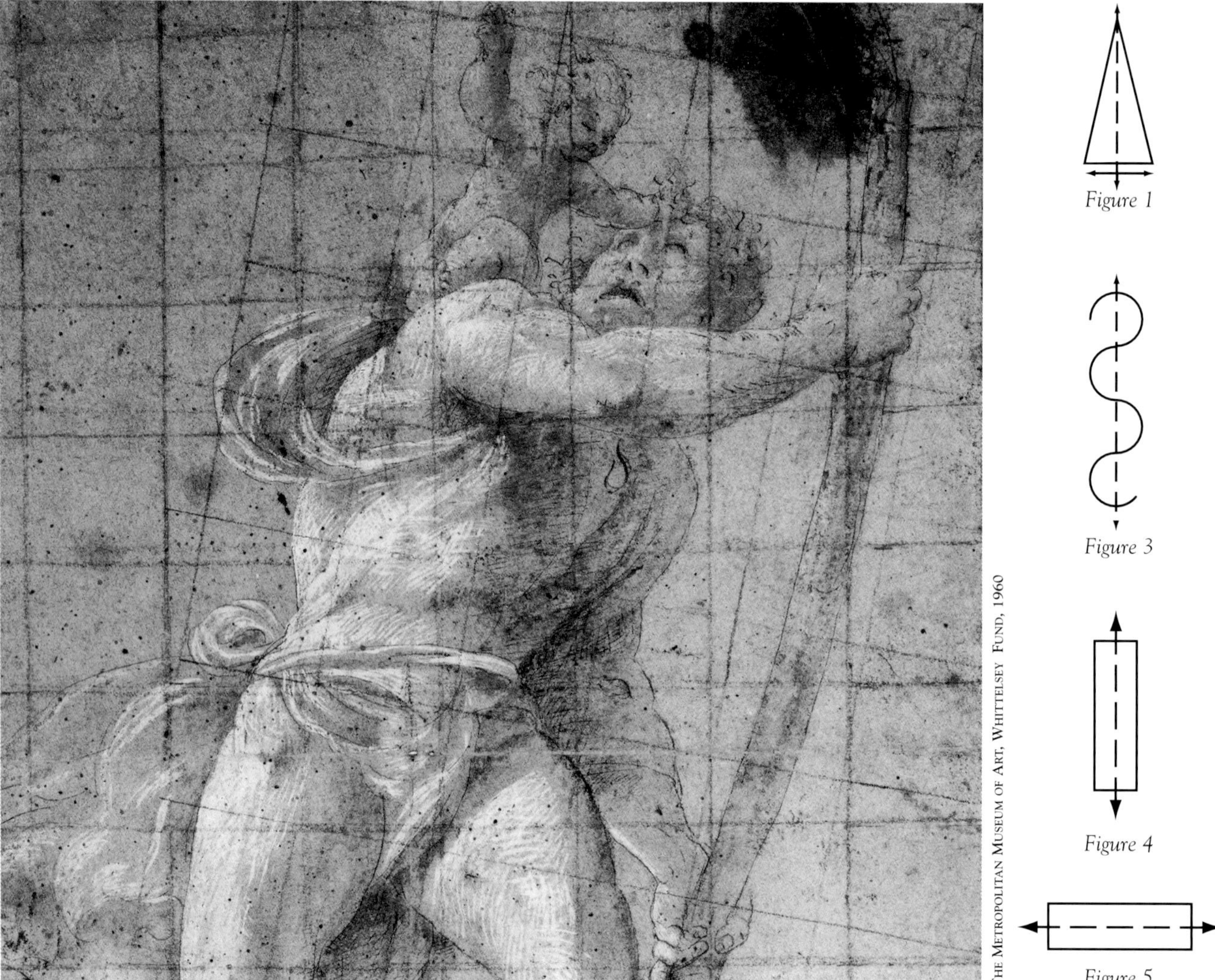

Figure 1

Figure 3

Figure 4

Figure 5

The Metropolitan Museum of Art, Whittelsey Fund, 1960

Figure 2. PORDENONE, ST. CHRISTOPHER (Detail)

point has no structural axis, it does have a visual function. When two or more points are placed in a picture plane, each of them may become stable, or less unstable. Certain combinations of points and lines can produce shape.

D. Size: The size of shapes is a very important characteristic in art. There can be different sizes of the same shapes. Through the differences of their appearance one can create patterns of great aesthetic interest.

E. Orientation: Orientation or position of shape in the picture plane, just as size, is independent of the character of the boundary and structural axes. Orientation determines the direction of the structural axes. Let us take, for example, a rectangle which is one inch in width and ten inches long. If we stand the rectangle in the visual picture plane with the one-inch side up, we have a structural axis of a strong vertical with a clear up and down direction (*Figure 4*). When the rectangle rests on the ten inch side, we have a change in direction in the structural axis (*Figure 5*). It now has a horizontal direction from side to side. In spite of the shift of position of a rectangle within the picture plane it is still recognized as being rectangular even though there is a radical change in the direction of the structural axis. The artist can keep boundaries and sizes constant and change the orientation of the shape in order to produce a variety of different directions of structural axes. The student can also combine changes in size and orientation while keeping the same shape.

Identical shapes can be rendered differently thereby giving each its own individual character. For example, a series of triangles, all of the same size, orientation, and structural character can all appear different due to a different linear character, style, or whether it has been drawn with a pencil, crayon, or painted with a brush.

F. Knowledge, Past Experience, and the Nature of Shape: In representational kinds of paintings to some degree, our past experience and knowledge come into play. For example, if a painter indicates on a canvas some windows, just a door, and a chimney above it, we do not see these as isolated and pure shapes. Our knowledge and past experience of seeing many houses makes us identify these individual shapes as belonging to a house. We associate therefore a mental image derived from past experience with these shapes, which do not physically represent a complete house on the picture plane. However, every "realistic representation" can be "reduced" to fundamental shape properties.

The Nature And Character of Brightness

Brightness is the degree of lightness (or whiteness) or darkness within a given shape or area. The word "value" is sometimes used to describe this. We believe brightness is a more descriptive term and it is generally used by experts to define this factor. Usually artists use the full range of brightness in their works of art from the lightest to the darkest. Many works of art have been done basically with just brightness and shapes such as drawings, etchings, lithographs and even paintings, the most famous example of this in modern times is Pablo Picasso's "Guernica", which is completely done in different brightnesses of grays, black and white (*Figure 127*).

The Nature and Character of Color

Every artist recognizes the importance of understanding the nature, characteristics and use of color in works of art. It is also important in the understanding, appreciation and the viewing of works of art. We shall list and describe the major characteristics of color:

1. *Hue*: Hue is a function of wavelength which produces a color quality such as red, yellow or blue. Black and white are not considered hues but are brightnesses. Red, blue and yellow are classed as the primary hues in art because no other combination of hues can produce them. Secondary hues are produced by a combination of primary colors: Red plus yellow yields orange, yellow plus blue yields green and blue plus red yields violet. By combining the different hues with different brightnesses the full range of colors can be produced. In painting there are pigments of different kinds of reds, yellows and blues and the combination of any of these will produce the different kinds of secondary colors. Thus, different results will come from the combination say of cadmium red with cadmium yellow, as compared with the mixture of alizarin crimson, which is another red, with say Naples yellow. This subject of color mixture, however, is outside the scope of the present study.

2. *Saturation*: Saturation is defined as the degree or percentage of purity of hue. For example, a pure red can be distinguished visually from a red which is less saturated which contains a mixture of other colors: blue, yellow, etc., or an addition of white or black. We can think of a completely saturated red as 100% red and one which is not fully saturated as having a lower percentage, say a red containing 10% blue. Therefore, the red will be classed as 90% saturated.

3. *Brightness*: Any color has a certain degree of brightness. One can add white or black to alter the brightness of the color, which will also affect its saturation. Saturated colors have a natural brightness without any additions of white or black or gray. A yellow is very light and high in brightness as compared with pure red which is darker.

4. *Thermal Quality*: Colors can be classified in terms of warmth and coolness: red and yellow are called warm colors, while blue and green are called cool.

5. *Spatial Distance*: Colors by themselves can give an impression of their position in depth, or give us an illusion of depth on the picture plane. For example, red and yellow give us the impression of being nearer, while blue and green seem to lie back in visual space under equal conditions.

6. *Hard and Soft Colors*: Red and yellow are classified as hard colors where as blue and green are classed as soft colors. This classification plays an important part in organization which will be treated later on in this text.

Color Solid

We have referred above to the classifications of: 1. Hue 2. Saturation and 3. Brightness. Taken together they can determine the physical character of all colors. However, they must be thought of independently because each has its own effect on how the color will be experienced. If we were to organize an available wide range of different color samples into what seemed to be a natural sequence we would probably first consider hue. For example, we would separate the reds from the blues, or the yellows from the greens. Then we would arrange the different hues in a natural sequence for example, yellow will be followed by orange, then red, rather than having an unnatural arrangement of orange, yellow then red. This is because orange contains some yellow and some red and therefore lies between them.

Then we would arrange all the different brightnesses of all the different kinds of hues. For example, all the reds would be arranged from the lighter reds to the darker ones. Then this is to be followed by an arrangement according to saturation. That is, arranged from the richest to the poorest hues. Colors that are directly opposite one another on the color solid are known as complementaries. Examples of complementary colors would be red and green, or yellow and blue. This classification is often demonstrated on color solids or pyramids (*Figure* 6) such as that in the Ostwald system. With the aid of the concept of the color solid, the artist can clearly know how an individual color fits into the world of color.

Color and Brightness Contrast

It is a widely known fact that brightness and hues are influenced in varying degrees by their surroundings. It is for this reason that artists should not use isolated colors or physical measurements as the absolute standard in judging the visual nature in a work of art.

Brightness Contrast

For example, when we paint two squares of the same gray on separate larger squares, one white, the other black, the gray square that was placed on the white one will appear darker. This is due to the phenomenon of brightness contrast (*Figures 7 and* 8).

Color Contrast

Differently colored areas when placed next to one another will influence each other. This process is known as the lateral interaction of colors. If two gray shapes are painted on different colored squares, one red, the other blue, the one painted on the red square becomes tinged with blue green and the one on the blue square is tinged with orange. The color, we will notice, that results is always the complementary of the influencing color, in this case red and orange.

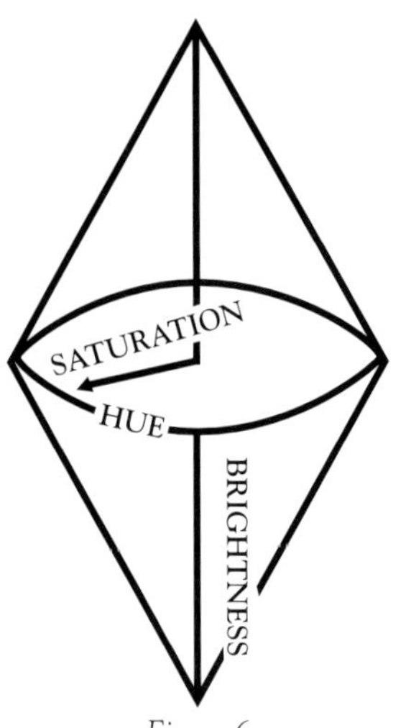

Figure 6

Figure 7

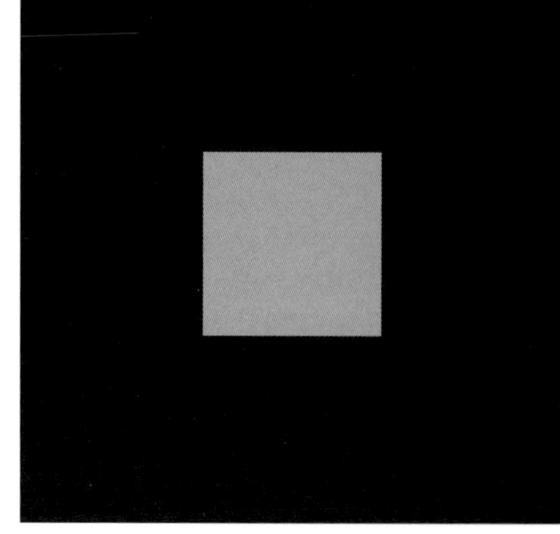

Figure 8

The most striking and vivid contrasts are obtained when the two colors that are being influenced are of the same brightness. The very sharp or abrupt contour of a shape prevents the activity of contrast effect. We can increase the interaction by softening the contour or increasing its ambiguity in various ways. We also can vary the degree of interaction by increasing or decreasing the distance between colors.

The following rules hold: 1. When the color areas are almost equal in size, the greater color contrast effect will be around the margins or edges. 2. The smaller one color area is in relation to the other, the greater the influence on the small color area will be. 3. The contrast effect will decrease with an increase of the distances between the areas of color.

Pre-outlined Exercises 1-6 (Sheet 1)

To gain some direct experiences on the nature of color contrast, complete the pre-outlined exercises (1-6). It is recommended that a set of tempera colors consisting of red, yellow, blue, green, black and white be used, which will be standard for most of the exercises performed in this course. You will notice that different areas which are to receive the different colors are indicated by letters: R represents red, Y for yellow and B for blue. Apply the tempera color smoothly and carefully. It is important to cover the lines indicating the boundaries, so that there will only be a contrast of one color area against the other, without linear contours.

The Principle of Structure

The two general concepts of a work of art are its structure and expression. Their proper understanding is an indispensable step towards a greater insight into the appreciation and creation of works of art.

The structure and expression in a work of art are produced by the use of the visual elements of shape, color and brightness. Shape and form are two distinct concepts. For example, in a line drawing that just indicates the boundary of an apple, the shape and form are identical. However, in a painting that combines all the visual elements of shape, color and brightness, they all contribute to the form of the apple.

The terms "forms" and "structures" (and also design and composition) are sometimes used interchangeably. We can distinguish between the two by saying that the structure of the work is the overall form, while individual portions of the work can be referred to as sub-structures or forms.

Classifications of Structure

Theoretically there can be an infinite number of works of art with different visual appearances, yet we can classify structure into two major categories: 1. Stable Structures and 2. Unstable Structures.

STABLE STRUCTURES: Stable structures are those that do not fluctuate but "stay put" visually. For example, a triangle is seen only as a triangle, or a circle as only a circle. (*Figure* 9).

MULTIPLE PATTERNS WITHIN A STRUCTURE: There are different degrees of dynamic flux of patterns. In some cases the pattern alternates between a few well-defined ways of being perceived as, for instance, a square that is halved by a horizontal line: the figure will be seen either as a square with a line across it or as a pair of rectangles, one on top of the other (*Figure 10*). Another example would be Picasso's "Head of a Woman" (*Figure 73*). It visually fluctuates between being seen as a representation of one head in full face and as a head in profile with another head behind it. In other cases ambiguity can be more complex. An almost unlimited number of patterns can be visually experienced in the same visual configuration. An ambiguous structure of this complex order (*Figure 11*) can be said to have an indefinite number of structural axes. One structural axis may clash with the others all being of equal dominance. Only when we see or have a strong structural axis or a set of axes (as in the triangle) do we get a more definite structural characteristic.

Method to Explore Stable and Unstable Structures

It can be very useful for the student and artist to explore the various degrees of stable and

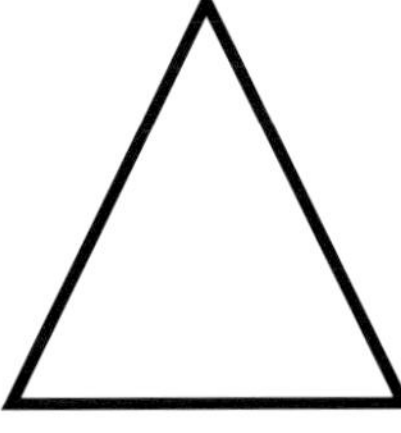

Figure 9

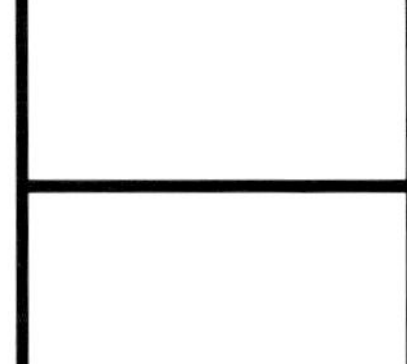

Figure 10

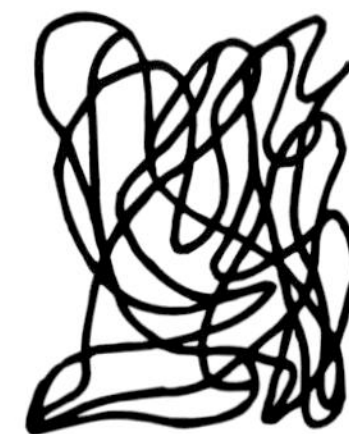

Figure 11

unstable structures because of their importance in the understanding of the nature of a work of art. We will describe what we believe to be an interesting, fruitful and sound approach. We shall outline the materials and procedure to use:

(A) MATERIALS: There is a wide variety in the choice of materials to be used. For example: pencil, ink, pastels, crayons, watercolors, tempera, oil colors, etc. They can be applied to paper or canvas.

(B) PROCEDURE: It is suggested that the student and artist make at least two ambiguous structures, one in monochrome and the other in color. Begin with the monochrome structure.

(1) The ambiguous structure can be established by scribbling or by either dripping or splattering ink or fluid paint. The alternate way is to carefully render or paint an ambiguous structure.

(2) Then study the structure by making various little sketches of some of the structural possibilities. This is one way the creative imagination can be stimulated. This fundamental procedure or method was suggested in the famous passage from Leonardo da Vinci's "Trattato Della Pittura" ("Treatise on Painting") where the master recommended that the artist and student, by studying and observing a confusion of forms in nature such as clouds, etc., can stir the creative imagination of the individual where one can see in them a variety of forms.

(3) The student should then choose one or two of the more interesting possibilities that were sketched and then make a final rendition.

The Relation of the Parts to the Whole Structure

It is of the utmost importance to clearly understand the relationship between the visual appearance of the general structure of a work and the "parts" within it. (Parts are defined as physically distinct or separate "pieces"). In *Figure 12*, a set of five identical parts are differently arranged than *Figure 13* thereby producing differently appearing structures. This is a clear demonstration of how identical parts can produce different visual structures through a difference in arrangement.

In *Figures 14*, *15*, and *16*, we see that a similarity of arrangement of visually dissimilar parts produce the same basic structure, that of a circle. *Figure 14* is one continuous line, *15* a series of lines, and *16* a series of squares. In music we can have a theme arranged for piano and also for full orchestra. When they are performed separately or at different times we can recognize a similarity in the overall thematic quality of the two arrangements despite the great differences in the kind of sounds produced by the various instruments. One is comprised of piano notes and the other strings, horns, percussion.

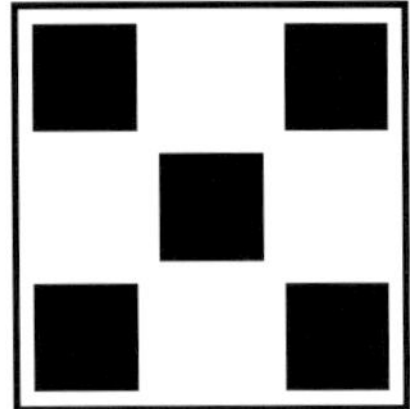

Figure 12

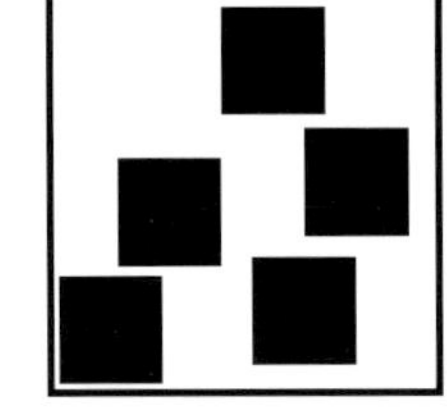

Figure 13

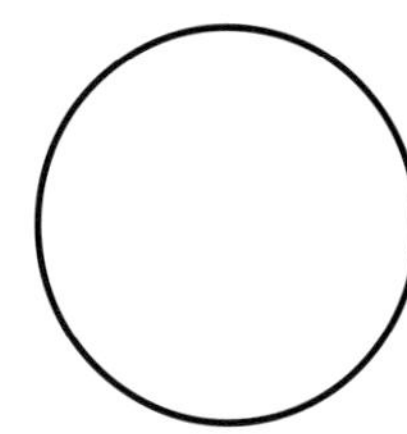

Figure 14

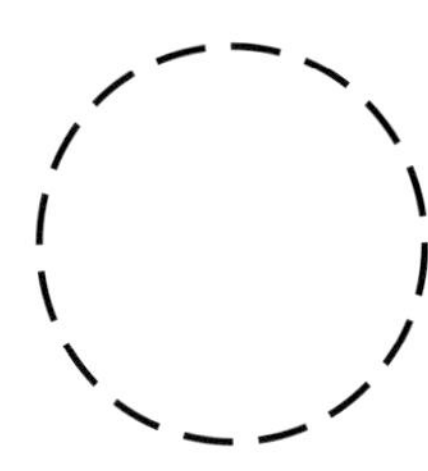

Figure 15

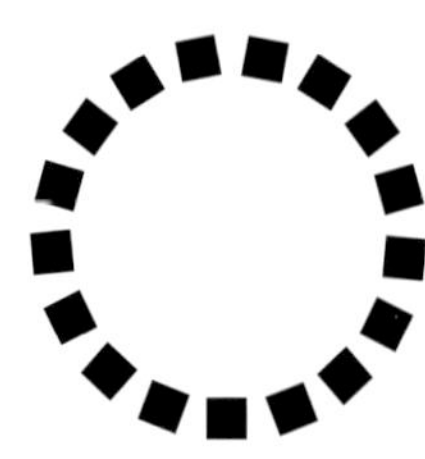

Figure 16

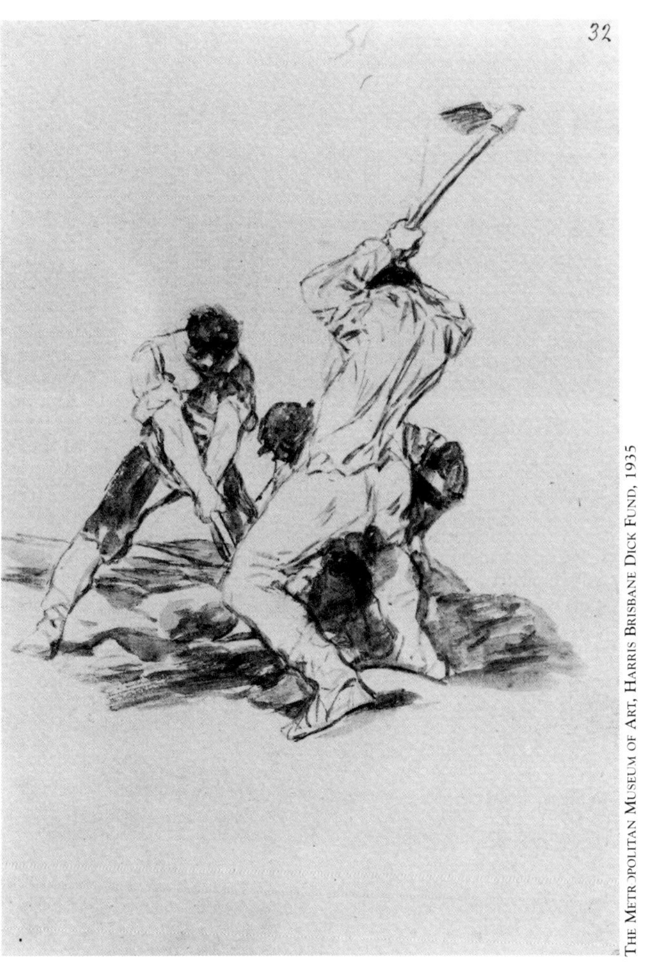

The Metropolitan Museum of Art, Harris Brisbane Dick Fund, 1935

Figure 17. GOYA, *THREE MEN DIGGING*

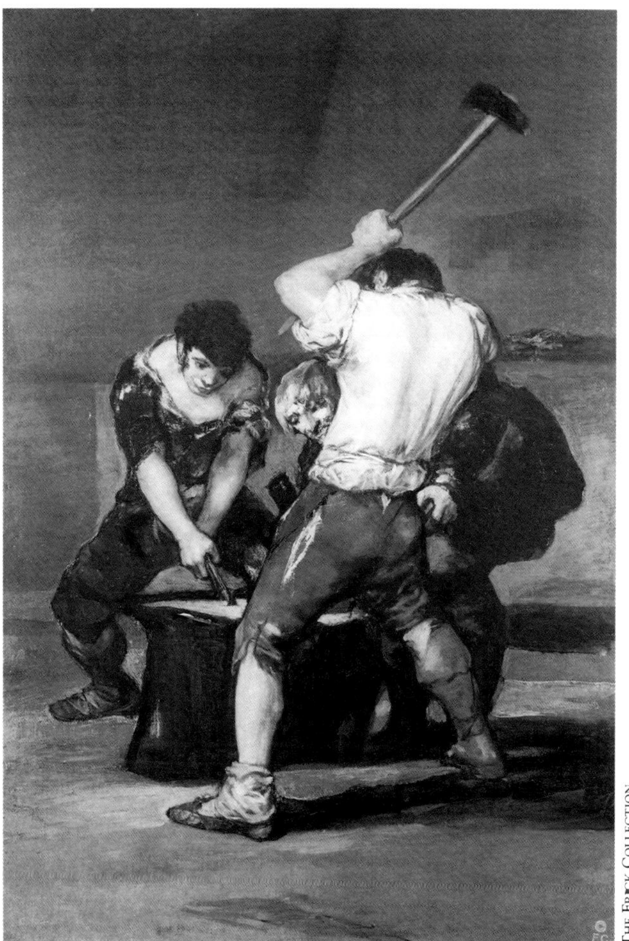

The Frick Collection

Figure 18. GOYA, *THE FORGE*

In the reproductions of two works by Francisco de Goya ("Three Men Digging" *Figure 17* and "The Forge" *Figure 18*) we recognize a general similarity in the visual structures of the work. This is true despite the various differences in activity, dress and posture of the individual figures.

There are numerous examples of works of art by different artists where there exist structural similarities. For example, Picasso's "Head of a Woman" (*Figure 19*) and Leonardo da Vinci's "Head of St. Mary" (*Figure 20*). If we especially examine the treatment of the eyes, mouth and nose, they reveal the same classic sculptural quality, as does the overall structural quality of the head. This contributes to the basic similarity of structure of the two heads. Additionally, we notice a clear stylistic difference between the two works. The Picasso drawing is executed simply and directly with distinctly indicated forms and greater contrast between the light and dark areas. Leonardo, on the other hand, gives us a painterly rendition through carefully gradations of shading.

In the two Goya works we have a similarity of structure with a basic consistency of style. In the Picasso and da Vinci works, we have a structural similarity with an entirely different stylistic character and with hundreds of years between them. This fact clearly illustrates that the concept of structure is highly universal and transcends differences in style and historical period.

We can conclude that we can never fully understand the nature of the structure in a work of art by a mere isolated analysis of the separate parts. We see that it is best understood through the nature of the arrangement of the parts.

The Purposeful Function of the Structure

The structure can be considered as a general plan that functions as a guide or framework within which the artist creates or develops the specific work of art. In *Figure 21* we observe that the arrangement of the dark circles has produced

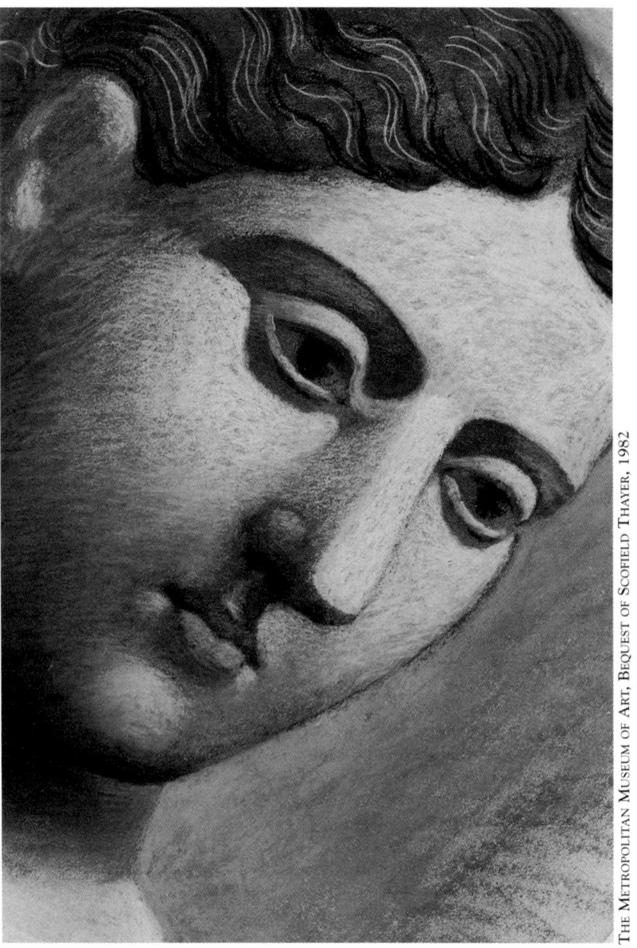

The Metropolitan Museum of Art, Bequest of Scofield Thayer, 1982

Figure 19. PICASSO, HEAD OF A WOMAN

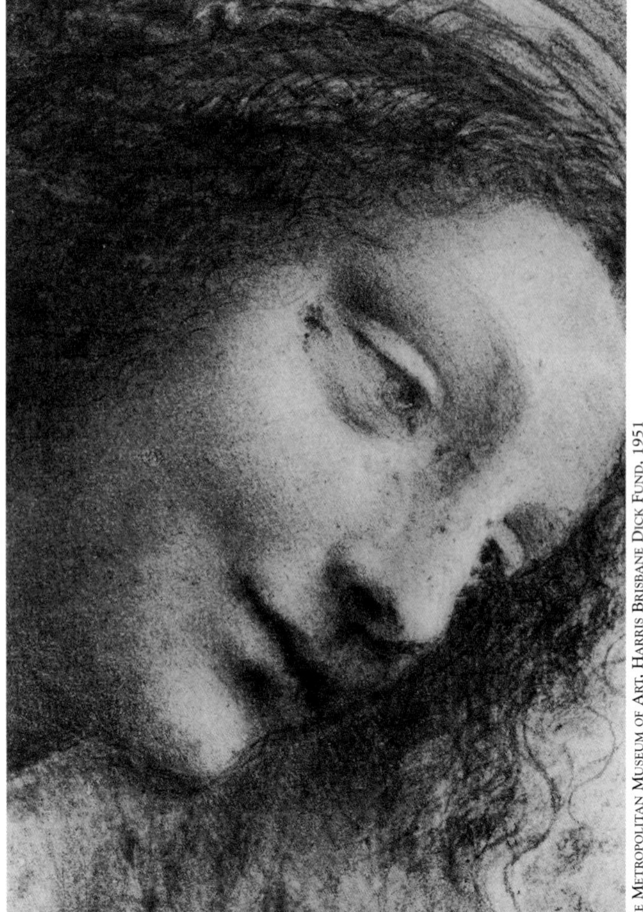

The Metropolitan Museum of Art, Harris Brisbane Dick Fund, 1951

Figure 20. LEONARDO DA VINCI, HEAD OF THE VIRGIN

the form of a triangle. We can consider *Figure 21* as a guide to the construction of *Figure 22* which represents a point or stage in the process of the creation of a work of art. After establishing the placement of forms A and B, comes the choice as to where the next square will be placed. Let us imagine that there are two possible locations for the square: C and D. If the square form is placed in position D the resulting form is a straight line. When placed in position C the form of a triangle is established. As we can see, this is a very simple and basic demonstration. *Figure 21* employs circles while 22 uses squares and yet both figures produce a triangle. This clearly illustrates that the "plan" of *Figure 21* did not guide the choice of the parts, but the arrangement of whatever parts were used.

To further clarify this important aspect of the concept of structure let us again refer to the Goya drawing and painting. One perhaps might say that since the drawing had already achieved the general structural and expressive character of the work there was not logical need for Goya to execute the painting, but the painting was done. The reason becomes clear if we think of the visual structure of the drawing as having the purposeful function as described in the example above. Goya used the drawing as a general guide for the creation of the painting, "The Forge." Goya's central purpose or motivation was not to merely repeat the overall similarity of structure but to create another work of art expressing the structure in a different manner. As we have

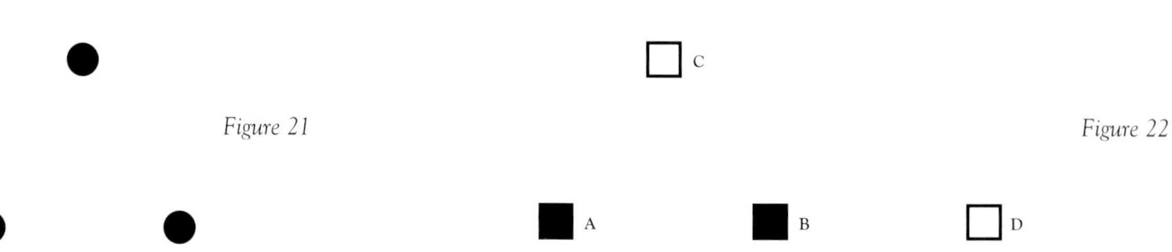

Figure 21

Figure 22

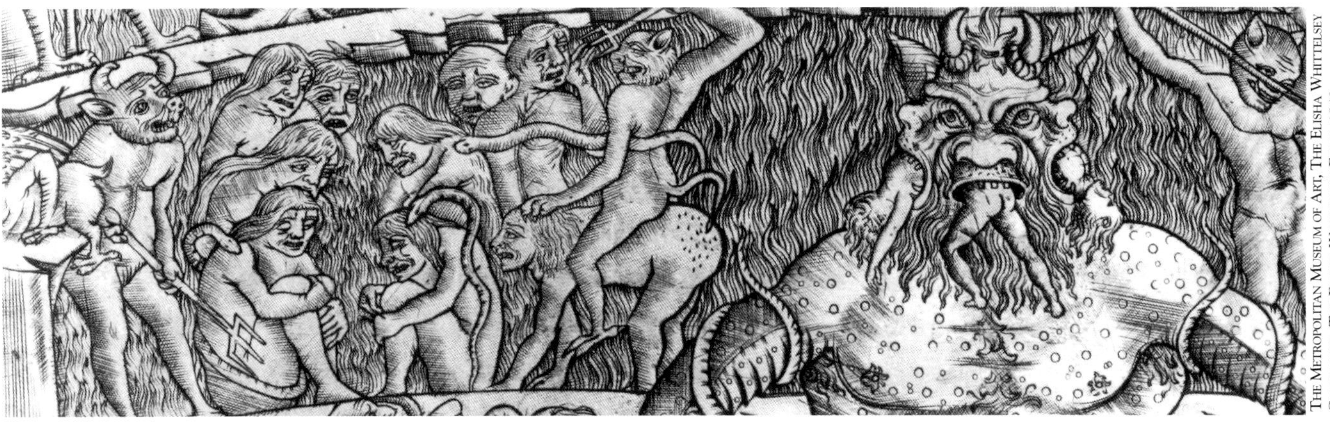

The Metropolitan Museum of Art, The Elisha Whittelsey Collection, The Elisha Whittelsey Fund, 1949

Figure 23. INFERNO ACCORDING TO DANTE, AFTER FRESCO IN CAMPO SANTO PISA FLORENTINE SCHOOL (Detail)

already seen, we can have many different forms (and renditions of forms, as in this case) arranged to produce basically similar structures.

Fundamentally, the artist is concerned with the development of a "general" structure - with selection of particular parts that can best express the artist's intention.

The Principle of Expression

We shall endeavor to show throughout this study the importance of expression in a work of art. We wish to show that the very foundation of art is rooted in expression. The French master, Henri Matisse, said that above all, what he was after was expression through the arrangements of the different parts in the total composition.

Expression is one aspect of what, in a larger sense, is called meaning. There are five basic levels of meaning. The first four are based on the beholder's or the individual's personal identification with the work, through verbal associations and meanings and past experience. This is based on Erwin Panofsky's method of iconographical analysis found in his *Studies of Iconology*, 1939.

1. *Individual Identification with the Work of Art*: The beholder can look at a work and associate his own personal experience and feelings with it and thereby enrich his aesthetic experience. The artist can project into the work his own particular feelings and ideas and experiences about the subject. It is a common experience among persons attending a film, play, or reading a book to have a strong personal identification with one or a number of characters in the story, which heightens the aesthetic experience. Theodor Lipps called this phenomenon "empathy". Empathy applies to music as well as painting.

2. *Experience with Everyday Objects and Events*: We can recognize a tree, a house, a human body, and its gestures and movements through our past experience. This refers exclusively to representational types of art, which attempt to aesthetically depict physical reality. This has been of great interest to many artists. Leon Battista Alberti's "Della Pittura", the first modern treatise on painting which appeared in Florence in 1435-36, contains advice to artists to study the full range of human facial and bodily movements and expression, so they can learn how to represent them.

3. *Illustrations of Stories*: Many artists have based great works of art on the Bible, mythology and other literary sources. The understanding of the artist's intentions is aided by a reading of the sources.

We have reproduced a detail of a fifteenth century engraving which illustrates a scene from the Inferno from Dante's "Divine Comedy". It shows the demons punishing the damned souls with the flames filling the background (*Figure 23*).

4. *Meaning on a Deeper Level*: Every work of art contains intangible factors which involve contributions of the subconscious mind. They are projections of the mind and personality of the artist, and reflect the influence of the historical period in which the artist worked or works. This is a deeper and more complicated part of the meaning and association embedded in a work of art. For if one paints a picture of the same subject matter in the 20th century as an artist did in the

15th century the result will be completely different owing to an entirely different set of intangible factors, and will result in different associations and meanings. For example, the famous passage from "The 17th Devotion" written by John Donne, in the 17th century, "no man is an island, entire of itself" - had a particular meaning for the poet, which was mainly spiritual. Owing to the shift of historical events, the meaning of the passage has shifted also. It has retained its basic spiritual quality, but it now has been associated with more diversified meaning, in the framework of our current history.

A parallel can be found within the progress of one's own life. We have at one time or another reacted differently to a similar event which may have occurred years before. For our idea, evaluation or reaction to second or repeated experiences of the same film, book or painting can change. Our appreciation of the work can grow or our previous judgment can be reversed. This has been determined by the development of the general nature of the mind and personality of the individual that has been taking place since the last similar experience.

Paul Cezanne in a letter he wrote in 1905 referred to the artist's relation to the past stating that the Louvre is the book from which the artist learns to read. He went on to say one must free himself of the past, to express himself according to his own personal temperament. This does not necessarily imply that the subject matter and the many different styles of the past cannot be adapted or transformed into a new kind of art form in the terms of the artist's individual personality and artistic aims which are very important factors. For Cezanne used the subject matter of the past (landscapes, still lifes and the human figure) and transformed it. As he said in another letter in 1905, the artist must try to add another link in the chain of art history, which Cezanne most definitely accomplished.

5. *Pure Artistic Expression (or Visual Expression)*: We now come to the fifth and most important level of meaning, namely, to what can be considered as pure, artistic expression, directly derived from the visual nature of the structure of the work of art. This pure artistic expression is that with which the artist is deeply concerned. Stories, verbal meanings, and personal identifications serve to embellish and make the work of art more interesting to some; but they are not as deeply rooted in art as the kind of pure visual expression with which we shall now deal. If we draw or paint a straight vertical line on a canvas or piece of paper, we will realize that the line has a definite forceful expression. However, when we change the orientation of the straight line and give it a horizontal direction, the resulting expression is peaceful or restful. We see then that a change of orientation of the same line produces a different expression. Orientation, as we said earlier, affects the structural direction of a line or shape, a purely visual characteristic. We see now that the change of orientation or position also changes its expression. This change of expression from the vertical to the horizontal line is largely independent of any particular meaning, past experience, stories or personal identification. It is strictly derived from visual experience. Rudolf Arnheim developed the gestalt theory of structural expression.

To clarify this independence of expression from past experience, we will give the following example. We might say that a vertical line reminds us of a strong, sturdy building, built very solidly such as the Empire State Building. If we compare it to a long, moving train traveling over a vast expanse, we know from past experience that physically the train is just as strong and sturdy as is the Empire State Building. Yet it is visually horizontal, and therefore it expresses a more peaceful appearance, as compared to the strong vertical of the building. We thus realize that the knowledge of the physical characteristics of the objects we observe is independent of the basic visual expression. This particular case of shift of expression due to change in orientation may be based on our sense of gravity. But we will show that expression is basically rooted in the visual structure of the work of art, and goes beyond a sense of gravity. If we compare the detail of the Vincent Van Gogh (*Figure 24*) "Cypresses" with that from the diptych by Van Eyck (*Figure 25*) of the panel representing "The Last Judgment", we might notice a similarity of structure. The brushwork which Van Gogh used in representing the foliage of the tree may be said to be somewhat similar to the arrangement of the figures of the damned souls in the Van Eyck. There is structur-

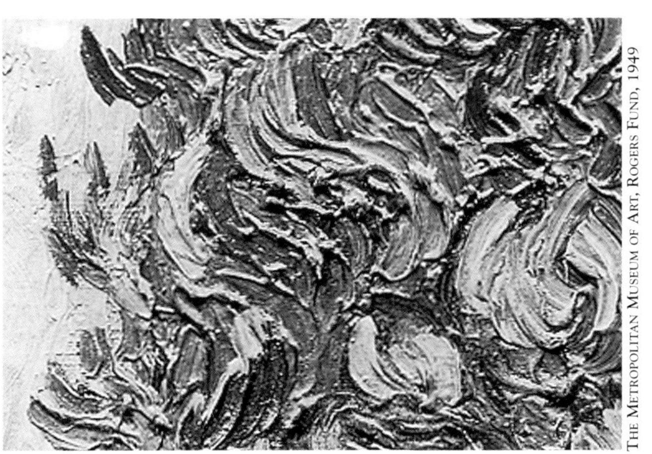

THE METROPOLITAN MUSEUM OF ART, ROGERS FUND, 1949

Figure 24. VAN GOGH, CYPRESSES (Detail)

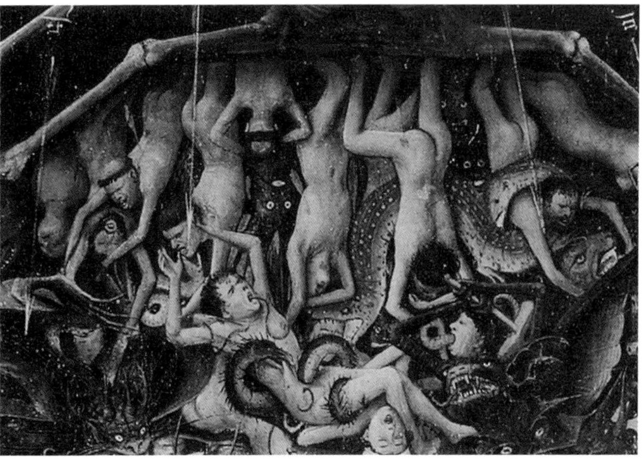

THE METROPOLITAN MUSEUM OF ART, FLETCHER FUND, 1933

Figure 25. JAN VAN EYCK, THE LAST JUDGMENT (Detail)

al similarity, yet the particular shapes are quite different. One picture represents realistic figures, derived from Van Eyck's motivation to depict a religious theme which was widely interpreted in Northern Europe in the 15th century. Whereas, Van Gogh wanted to represent nature in terms of his own point of view, personality, etc. We can see that there is a similarity of expression, even though the sources or motivations are entirely different and the particular shapes are different as well. But the same agitated feeling is conveyed in the two works. Therefore, we can conclude that mere knowledge of figures in the Van Eyck work, or the tree in the Van Gogh, or the Empire State Building, or the trains, are not the carrier by themselves of the basic visual expression, but the expression stems from the pure visual arrangement of forms and their orientation in the picture plane. Shape, brightness and color can play an equally important role in the formation of expressive quality through structure.

A valuable approach in understanding the nature of the general expression of a work of art is to study the relationship between the five different levels of expression. For example, let us consider the relationship between the meaning, understood with reference to our past experience, and knowledge, and the nature of pure artistic expression derived from the visual structure. Let us compare the details shown in *Figures 23* and 25. In these works both the artists of the engraving and Van Eyck had the same basic intention to depict damned souls in agony.

If we take a sheet of tracing paper, place it over the reproductions, and make a simplified outline of the major forms, then, after carefully studying it, we should be able to indicate the dominant structural axes (or visual directions of the forms). This kind of analysis will minimize the reference to our past experience and knowledge, and it will reveal the basic visual structure and its expression in the works. We will observe that in the Van Eyck the expression of the structure complements the meaning on the level of past experience and knowledge far greater than in the engraving.

The artist and student can more clearly understand the nature and range of pure artistic expression as described in this section, by simply drawing or painting pure forms using some or all of the visual elements to express extreme moods such as gloom and gaiety, or calm and turbulence. An interesting exercise for the artist and student is to listen to an appropriately chosen musical piece and attempt a visual representation with pure form of the mood expressed by the music. After this, the artist can manipulate the visual forms more easily to represent the more subtle expressions besides the extremes of moods. We have seen in the above text how expression is embedded in the pure visual character of the structure. We can therefore conclude that any exploration of expression will also widen our understanding of structure since the two factors are interconnected.

ART AND REALITY

We have already in the previous section demonstrated that pure artistic expression is largely independent of our past experience and knowledge of physical reality. Our understanding of art can be widened through the further clarifi-

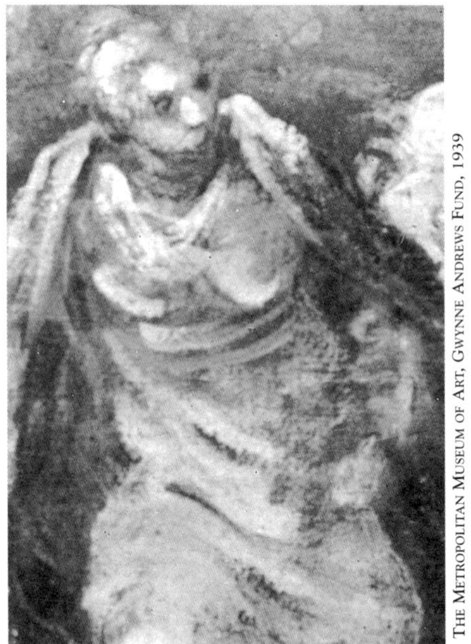

THE METROPOLITAN MUSEUM OF ART, GWYNNE ANDREWS FUND, 1939

Figure 26. TINTORETTO, THE FINDING OF MOSES (Detail)

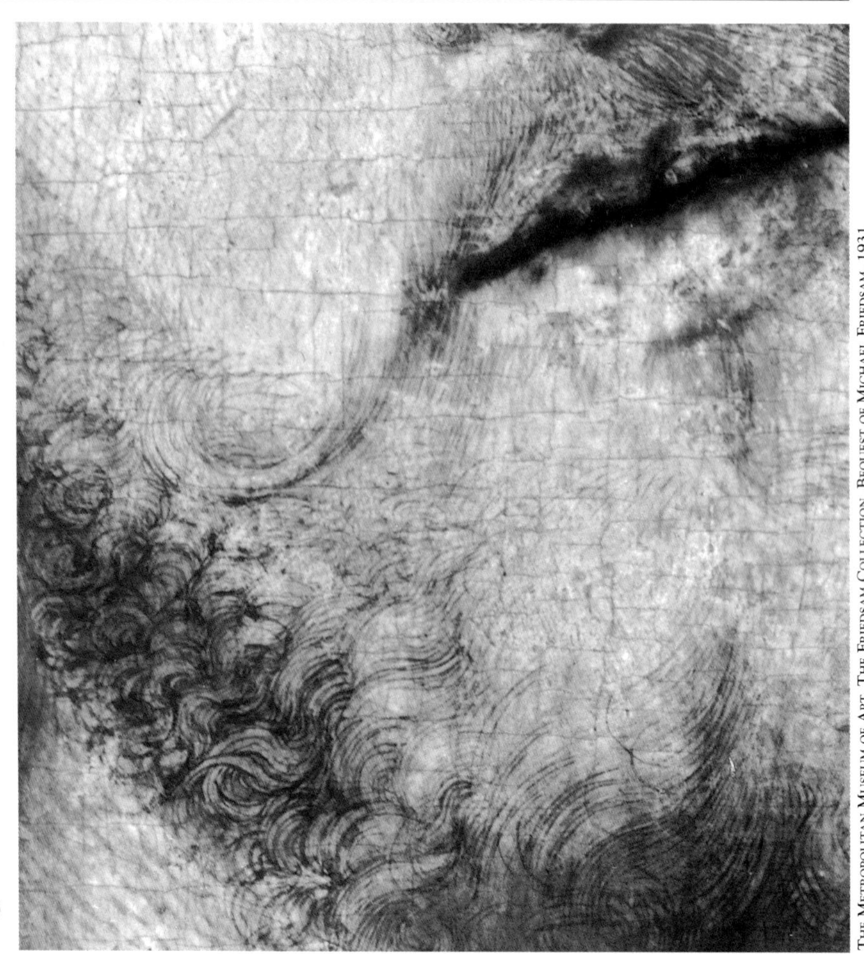

THE METROPOLITAN MUSEUM OF ART, THE FRIEDSAM COLLECTION, BEQUEST OF MICHAEL FRIEDSAM, 1931

Figure 27. DURER, SALVATOR MUNDI (Detail)

cation of the basic distinction between art and reality. We have reproduced the almost exact size of a detail of a figure from Tintoretto's "The Finding of Moses" (*Figure 26*). In the broadest sense of the term, Tintoretto is considered a realistic artist. The detail represents Tintoretto's interpretation of realistic forms. If we examine it closely and objectively we come to realize how different it appears than a realistic form of a human figure. It is far from a photographic representation. Here we have a clear distinction then, between the artist's interpretation of a real object and the nature of the object itself. The cause of this difference is that a work of art is a creation of man, not of nature. This is quite evident because a work of art reflects the individual personality and mind of the artist who created it and the historical period in which he worked or works.

A work of art has an artistic style that may be compared to a person's handwriting which has a distinctly individual character. Precisely this type of a phenomenon is not found in nature. If we examine the detail from Albrecht Durer's "Salvator Mundi" (*Figure 27*) which appears to be a far more realistic interpretation than the Tintoretto, we see that the curls are very neatly organized. If we compare it to a beard as it would appear in reality, we find there is a great deal of difference. In reality not every single hair is exactly arranged as it is in the Durer work. The master did not attempt or find it necessary to represent every single hair of the real beard. He selected certain forms to achieve the visual effect. Selection is an important factor in defining the relationship between art and reality. There does exist a kind of order in nature, also, such as a well organized geometric pattern of snail shells and snow flakes. But these shapes do not reflect an individual artist's personality, mind and historical framework.

Order in art is derived from a basic human motivation, need or urge. We all experience the desire to order, when we organize our desks, gardens, or arrange the furniture in a room to achieve a pleasing effect. This sense of order is carried into the realm of art in a special way. The formal principles on which art is based can be traced directly to this basic human desire for order. One of the differences between ordering a room and the painting of a room is this: the vase you might put on the table is held there by gravity; but when the artist represents it on canvas, the vase is held there exclusively by a specific visual order, which is independent of physical gravity. This use of representational elements in art does not imply that the artist copies nature mechanically: he orders it in visual terms in accordance with his artistic aims.

Collage and Reality

In 1912 the important invention of collage was made. It was a development of the Cubistic movement. The Cubists radically departed from the representation of nature of the physical world around them by taking it apart and organizing it in purely visual terms rather than copying it.

Collages are works of art that are made up of pasted down strips of newspaper, cloth and other elements which we find in everyday life. These varied materials are cut into different shapes and arranged in an artistic effect. This can be observed in Pablo Picasso's "Man With a Hat" (*Figure 28*) done in December 1912 which combines the use of charcoal, ink and pasted paper.

If we were to pin the front page of a newspaper on a wall, its original function would be preserved; that is, we would tend to read it and not view it as a work of art. But when it is cut into a definite shape and integrated into an artistic order as in the Picasso work the original purpose tends to be subordinated. It now functions in an order that is apart from the type of order that is found in reality. (The causes of this will be treated in the section on direction).

We have clearly demonstrated with the Picasso, Durer and Tintoretto examples, how artistic order is distinct from the order found in reality. The nature of this artistic order is the major subject of this course.

The Principle of Unity Within Variety

There are three fundamental principles that define the special visual and expressive order of a work of art: (1) the principle of unity within variety, (2) the principle of balance, and (3) the principle of hierarchy. These principles distinguish a work of art from our everyday visual experience.

The purpose of the principle of unity within variety is to organize the different forms in a work of art into an organized, pleasing structure.

We can not treat unity within variety purely on the level of structure or purely on the expressive level. As we have seen, we can not separate pure artistic expression from the visual structure which produces it.

The foundation on which the principle of unity within variety rests can best be understood by a simple demonstration. If one could continually pronounce the same word in a similar manner with equal time intervals between them until one begins to clearly experience monotony, then one may begin to sense a natural tendency to introduce variations in pronunciation and create a more varied rhythm. In this way, one can subdue or even eliminate the expression of monotony and produce a more pleasing expression. If one goes on to the other extreme by making excessive variations, the expression of confusion will result. The natural tendency will be toward more balance between similar visual qualities which creates unity and dissimilarity which creates variety.

The painting by Claude Monet "The Four Trees", formerly "The Poplars" (*Figure 29*) is a fine example that clearly demonstrates the nature of unity within variety in a work of art. In this work we have four similar trees on a bank of a river with their reflections in the water. Within this overall similarity, we also have a number of variations. For instance, the trees are not equally spaced and are shaped differently. There are also variations in the amount and arrangement of the foliage on each tree. We can see how Monet balances the degree of unity and variety of visual forms, and this avoids the expression of excessive unity or variety.

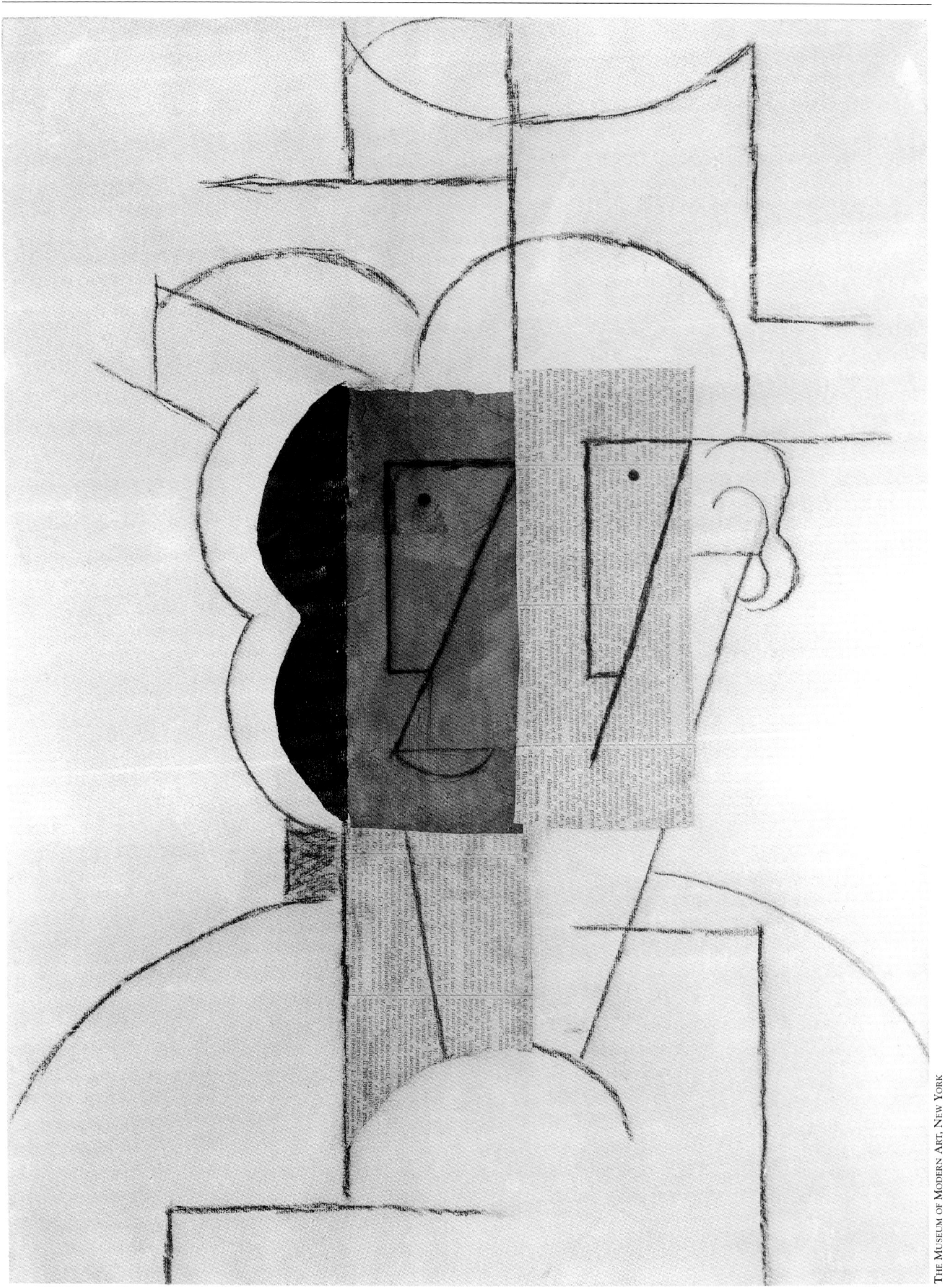

THE MUSEUM OF MODERN ART, NEW YORK

Figure 28. PICASSO, MAN WITH A HAT *(after December 3, 1912; pasted paper, charcoal and ink on paper, 24 1/2 x 18 5/8")*

Cohesive and Segregating Forces

To more fully understand the nature of artistic order it will be necessary to refer to the manner in which we "see". The character of our visual experience is a result of the electro-chemical processes in the sector of the brain that deals with seeing. These processes can be explained by what are called "cohesive" and "segregating" forces. They function in a definite way and the general principles were described in 1923 by Max Wertheimer, the famous formulator of the Gestalt theory. He was the first to classify them systematically although artists have been using them intuitively for centuries. Generally speaking, when forms are near each other or share similar visual properties, cohesive forces are produced in the brain which visually group or unify the forms to some degree. Segregating forces are produced when forms are distinctly separate or have dissimilar visual properties. These segregating forces visually "separate" the forms from one another. In other words, the cohesive forces tend to attract visual forms while segregating forces tend to repel them.

It is a general rule that, as the cohesive forces increase, the segregating forces decrease, and vice versa. The cohesive forces are inversely proportional to the segregating forces. This is a very convenient way of thinking of these two principles, which produce unity within variety and affect the structure of the work.

Exercise in Creating a Pleasing Visual Order

At this point it can prove useful to perform a simple exercise which can generally reveal the students rapport with his innate tendency in creating a pleasing arrangement of forms. (However, as the course progresses, there can be a greater realization of the student's potential in this factor.) The artist's very particular visual and expressive intention in a work of art is fused with the natural tendency toward a pleasurable framework.

The materials which are used in this exercise are two 9" x 12" sheets of paper, a soft pencil and black and white tempera color. The task is to make a pleasing arrangement (from the individual's point of view) just using three black vertical and three black horizontal lines which are to touch the edges of the work. To aid in finding a satisfactory arrangement, make several small preparatory pencil sketches on the first sheet to be numbered in the order they are done. The black lines can vary in thickness and texture, or can be all uniform. The character of the black lines can be controlled or altered with the aid of white paint. After the exercise is completed both sheets should be signed and submitted to the teacher for study and evaluation. Each student's work can be ranked or categorized within the framework of the whole class. At one end the more regular or monotonous works are to be placed, and at the other end of the scale the works which express confusion. The mid-area will be the works which have pleasing arrangement of lines. The works then should be displayed along the wall for the whole class to study and briefly discuss.

The Factor of Nearness

The factors of organization were first classified by Wertheimer. They are the factors of nearness, similarity, direction and closure. A proper understanding of these factors will greatly aid the individual in mastering the principle of unity within variety.

The closer forms are in a picture space the greater is the degree of cohesive forces between them, and the greater the degree of unity. The further away from each other, the greater are the segregating forces thereby producing greater variety. In *Figure 30*, we have three differently spaced dots: A, B and C. The closer ones, A and B are grouped or organized to form a visual "unity" produced by the high degree of cohesive forces. Dot C is visually isolated due to the higher degree of segregating forces than cohesive forces between B and C. The segregating forces and the cohesive forces have determined the degree of unity and variety in the pattern of the dots experienced by the beholder.

We have reproduced Seurat's painting (*Figure 31*) of one of the final studies for "The Grande Jatte". If we look along the area where the shadow and light meet, we find on our left two people sitting down, a man and a woman, and to our right two women sitting on the edge

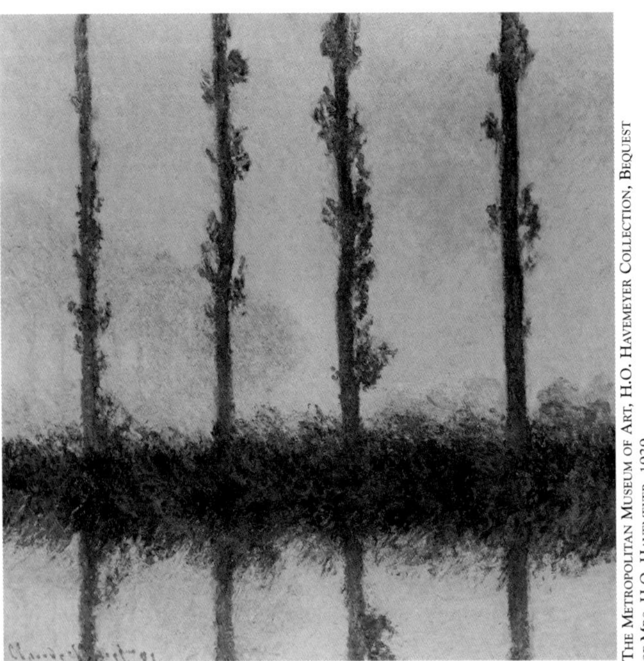

THE METROPOLITAN MUSEUM OF ART, H.O. HAVEMEYER COLLECTION, BEQUEST OF MRS. H.O. HAVEMEYER, 1929

Figure 29. MONET, THE FOUR TREES

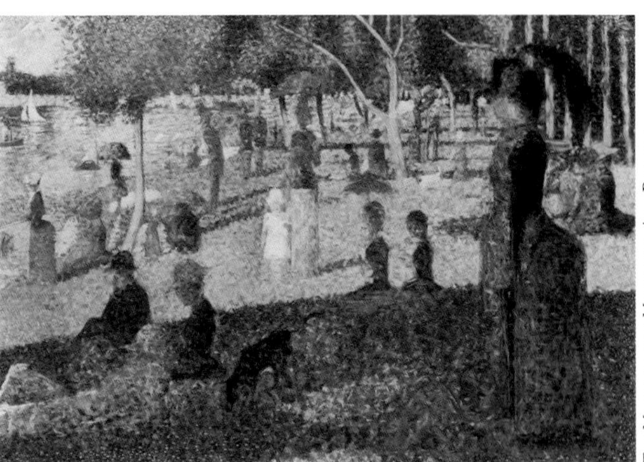

THE METROPOLITAN MUSEUM OF ART, BEQUEST OF SAM A. LEWISOHN, 1951

Figure 31. SEURAT,
Study for A SUNDAY ON LA GRANDE JATTE

A B C

Figure 30

of the shadow. The figures are grouped into two separate units. In between these two couples, we have a field of segregating forces, which visually separate these two units. Within each group of separate couples the cohesive forces are stronger, and that's what has unified these forms in the painting. One can simply make this analogy with the tapping of a pencil. Tap two sounds together quickly, then pause, then tap twice again, and you will see that it will form two separate units. Those closer together are heard together.

A fine example of the employment of the factor of nearness in contributing to cohesion of the work is found by comparing the final preparatory study (*Figure 32*) to the finished painting of "Les Demoiselles de Avignon" (*Figure 33*) done by Picasso in the spring of 1907. We observe in *Figure 33* how Picasso decreased the width of the work by reorganizing and modifying and compressing the figures closer together, producing higher cohesive forces between the forms as compared with *Figure 32*.

THE FACTOR OF SIMILARITY

A similarity of the characteristics and the properties of color, shape or brightness in a work can produce a high degree of cohesive forces, and unity of forms. A dissimilarity of visual properties will result in an increase in segregating forces producing variety. We observe in *Figures 34 - 37* that the forms are placed equally distant from each other. In *Figures 34* and *35*, we have different patterns created by the cohesive forces that visually connect the forms. For example, where the similar forms are placed horizontally (*Figure 34*) they create a unified horizontal pattern. In *Figures 36* and *37*, we have the same perpendicular arrangement of circular shapes, within which we have differently distributed brightnesses creating different dominant patterns. For example, in *Figure 36* the dark circles have created a triangle while in *Figure 37*, we have a right angle. In *Figures 36* and *37*, both the factors of nearness and similarity of shape have been subdued by the similarity of brightness which has created variety. One must be clearly aware, and the eye is the best judge, which patterns are more dominant or equal in dominance, with the aid of knowledge of these factors of structure.

UNITY AND VARIETY THROUGH SHAPE

In this little drawing of a man by Leonardo da Vinci (*Figure 38*), we observe how the artist organized the work through differences and similarities of shapes. The similar arched lines unify the profile of the forehead and the nose. We can see the similarity between the general form of the lower part of the nose and the chin, we see that the whole form of the mouth is repeated in the form of the eye, thereby producing cohesive forces, unifying these different areas. We can also

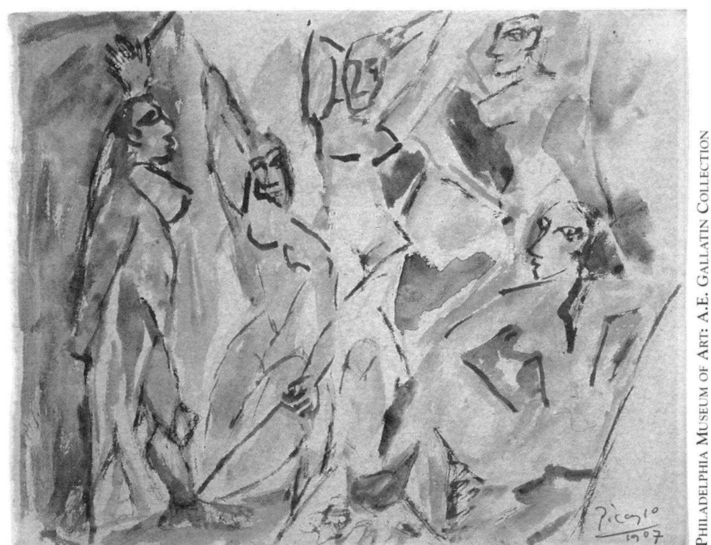

Philadelphia Museum of Art: A.E. Gallatin Collection

Figure 32. PICASSO, Study for THE YOUNG LADIES OF AVIGNON

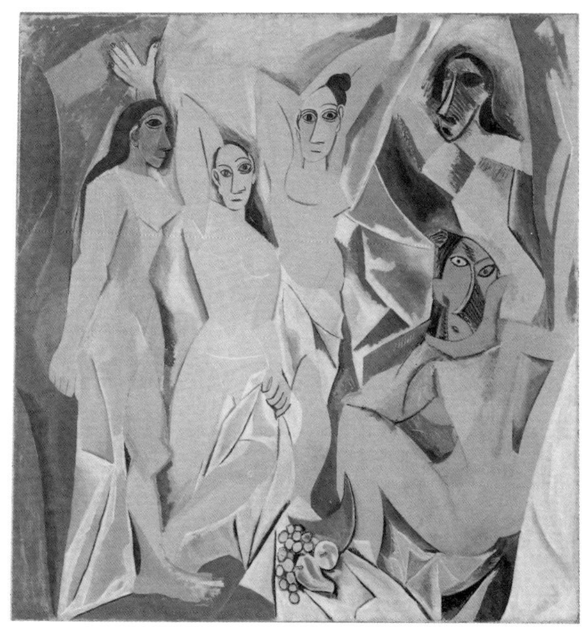

The Museum of Modern Art, New York. Acquired through the Lillie P. Bliss Bequest.

Figure 33. PICASSO, LES DEMOISELLES d'AVIGNON (June-July 1907, Oil on canvas, 8' x 7'8")

see how da Vinci achieved variety in the different ways, for example, by varying the sizes of the similar shapes of the eye and the mouth, and the nose and chin. The chin is not directly unified with the nose, it has the mouth between them. And the eye and the mouth which are similar have the nose intervening between them. The alternating of similar and dissimilar shapes contributes to the unity and variety in the work. Da Vinci also produced variety by the different shadings, the wrinkles on the face, and other little details. In even the smallest sketch, artists are concerned with the basic aim of having unity within variety to produce a pleasing aesthetic effect.

Unity Within Variety through Brightness and Color

In Picasso's "The Woman in White" (*Figure 39*), Picasso produced strong cohesive forces throughout the picture aiding the unification of the different forms in the work by a similarity of brightness. For example, the dress and flesh of the woman are light in brightness. He also brushed on a white glaze (which is a thin transparent veil of oil color) practically over the entire surface of the work, unifying the different shapes and colors which still contribute to the variety of the work. One can make experiments like this with colored cellophane, covering over many dissimilar shapes, and this solid film of one color or brightness will tend to unify it through its high cohesive forces, produced by the strong similarity of color or brightness.

One can analyze for himself how Henri Matisse (*Figure 40*) and Georges Rouault (*Figure 41*) achieve unity within variety. Observe how these artists organized similar and dissimilar forms within the two works. In studying and analyzing works of art, it has been found that tracing paper can prove quite useful. By placing it over the reproduction and carefully drawing the individual forms and patterns, in a simplified manner, indicating the major structural features. Different colored pencils or crayons can be used for indicating different patterns. This kind of analysis can be carried out with every reproduction in the book and can aid the student in following the text more carefully. The student should use all the information learned up to that point.

Scale of Visual Dominance of Forms

We see that in the da Vinci drawing, for example, the nose is more visually dominant than the chin, because of its larger size. (The factor of size alone is not always the determining factor in creating visual dominance. Other factors will be more fully discussed in the sections on the Principles of Balance and Hierarchy). One's eye is

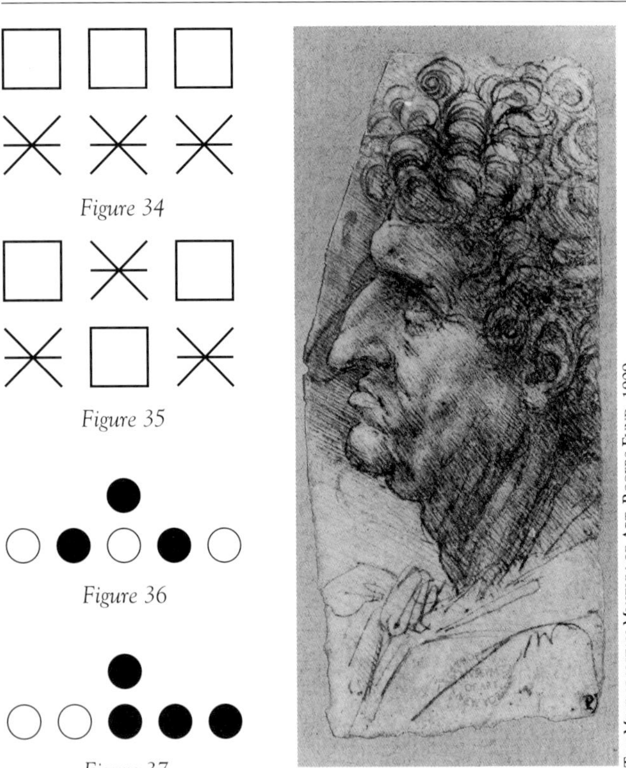

Figure 34

Figure 35

Figure 36

Figure 37

THE METROPOLITAN MUSEUM OF ART, ROGERS FUND, 1909

Figure 38. LEONARDO DA VINCI, HEAD OF A MAN IN PROFILE

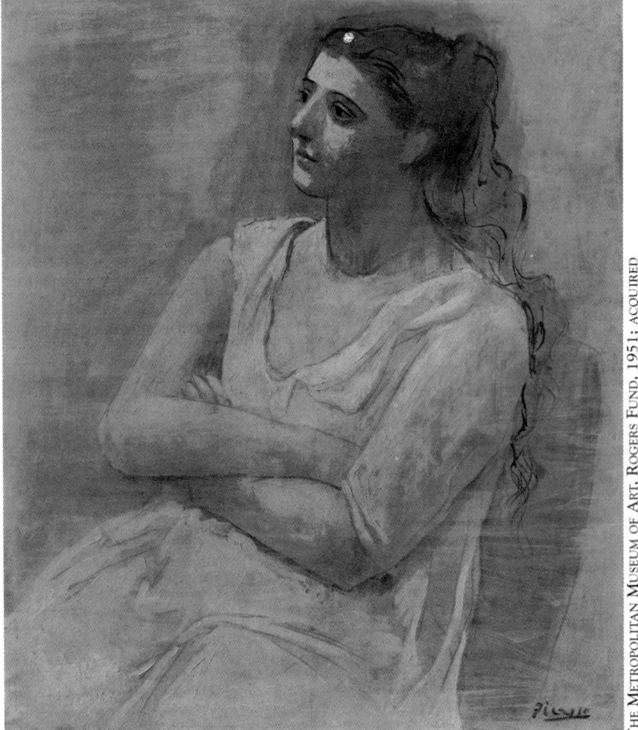

THE METROPOLITAN MUSEUM OF ART, ROGERS FUND, 1951; ACQUIRED FROM THE MUSEUM OF MODERN ART, LILLIE P. BLISS COLLECTION

Figure 39. PICASSO, WOMAN IN WHITE

the best judge in determining visual dominance, aided by the knowledge of the factors and principles of art.

The factor of the degree of visually dominant is an important factor of the principle of unity within variety. For generally speaking, works of art have one or few visually dominant forms or patterns (sometimes called the center of interest), arranged or organized with others of less visual dominances, or with patterns one less visually dominant than the other. Thus, the visual structure of a work is created that possesses a scale ranging from the most visually prominent patterns to those of lesser dominance. The range and number of visual patterns in this scale vary with the work and the individual artist's intentions. It must always be remembered that even the visual pattern of the least dominance is important in the work of art. For every detail of a work of art has a clearcut function in creating the total effect and a work of art should never have extraneous forms within it. The importance of the variety of visual dominance of forms in a work of art recalls what William Hogarth wrote in his famous treatise, "The Analysis of Beauty", published in 1753. He stated, "The art of composing well is no more than the art of varying well."

The Interplay Between Similarity and Nearness in Forming Unity and Variety

We shall now demonstrate, by using basic examples, the interplay or relation between the factor of similarity or dissimilarity of visual properties and the factor of nearness in the establishment of unity and variety. In *Figure 42*, we see how a similarity of shape and brightness (or color) and the equal space interval between the forms (the factor of nearness) produces a high degree of cohesive forces which unifies the four circles into a strong, single set of forms. In *Figure 43* and *Figure 44*, we can see how the unifying effect of the factor of nearness of forms can be subdued by the similarity and dissimilarity of shape, color or brightness. In *Figure 43*, the first and third circles are seen together while the second and fourth are grouped as a separate unit due to the similarity of brightness. In *Figure 44*, the two squares are grouped as a unit while the two circles form another, illustrating how a similarity of shape can unify forms independent of the nearness of the square and circular shapes. There is still a degree of unity of all the forms (*Figure 43*) due to the similarities of shape and nearness. This is also true of *Figure 44* as a result of the factor of nearness. One can find it useful to experi-

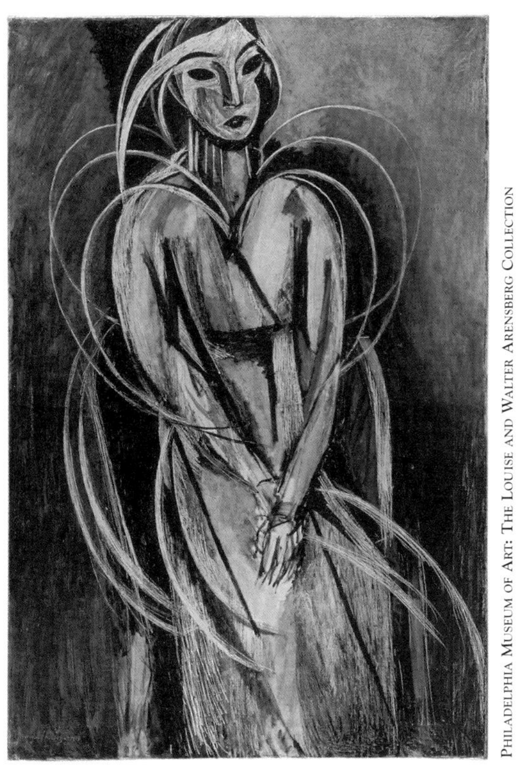

Philadelphia Museum of Art: The Louise and Walter Arensberg Collection

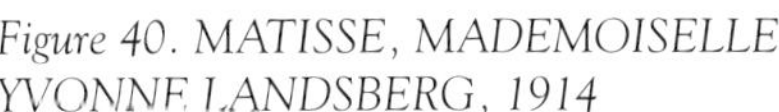

Figure 40. MATISSE, MADEMOISELLE YVONNE LANDSBERG, 1914

The New York Public Library

Figure 41. ROUAULT, PORTRAIT OF ANDRE SUARES

Figure 42

Figure 43

Figure 44

ment by varying the distances between the forms to observe the different degrees of unity and variety that are produced due to the various degrees of similarity or dissimilarity or nearness of the visual properties of forms.

It will be remembered that shape has different properties, such as boundary, structural axes, size and orientation. Color also has several different properties including hue, saturation, brightness and thermal quality. Forms can be unified through a similarity of these different properties of shape and color, and variety can be achieved through a dissimilarity of them.

THE FACTOR OF DIRECTION

The organization of similarity and dissimilarity of visual direction contributes to the production of unity and variety. If we would scribble a number of lines on a piece of paper, and then finally add one straight line through all the mass of scribble, we would see that the straight line forms a separate unit due to the similarity of a single direction against a background of very dissimilar arrangement of lines going in all different directions (*Figure* 45). It has also been called the factor of good continuation. This demonstrates how a similarity of direction can produce strong cohesive forces and form units or unity. It is seen as a single line, rather than part of a mass of scribbles. The difference between the single direction of the line and the many different directions of the scribbling produces segregating forces which result in a clear distinction between them.

The visual directions of a form create what Wassily Kandinsky has called "directed visual tension." This visual tension produces a sense of visual movement in a work of art. "Visual movement" in a work of art means simply visual direction; and therefore, cannot be compared to the physical motion, that we may witness in everyday life. Every work of art possesses some degree of visual tension or movements.

In the detail of a Greek vase (*Figure* 46) done in the 6th century B. C. which represents a footrace, we experience a sense of visual movement. This was achieved through purely visual arrangement of forms. The overlapping and repetition of basically similar forms of runner figures creates a visual rhythm. We also observe that there is a diminishing interval of space between the leading runner and the three figures behind him. This device creates a greater sense of visual movement than if the figures were equally

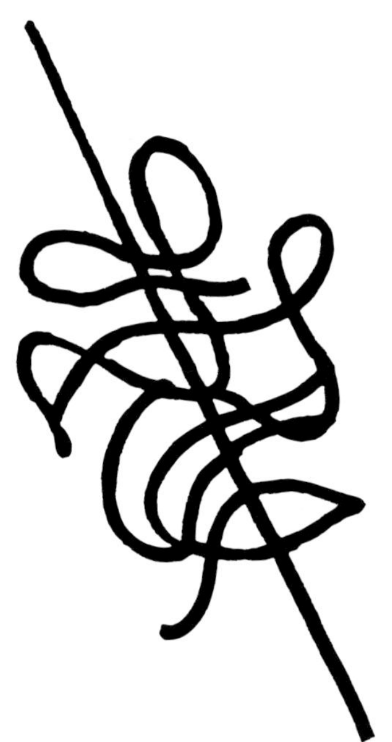

Figure 45

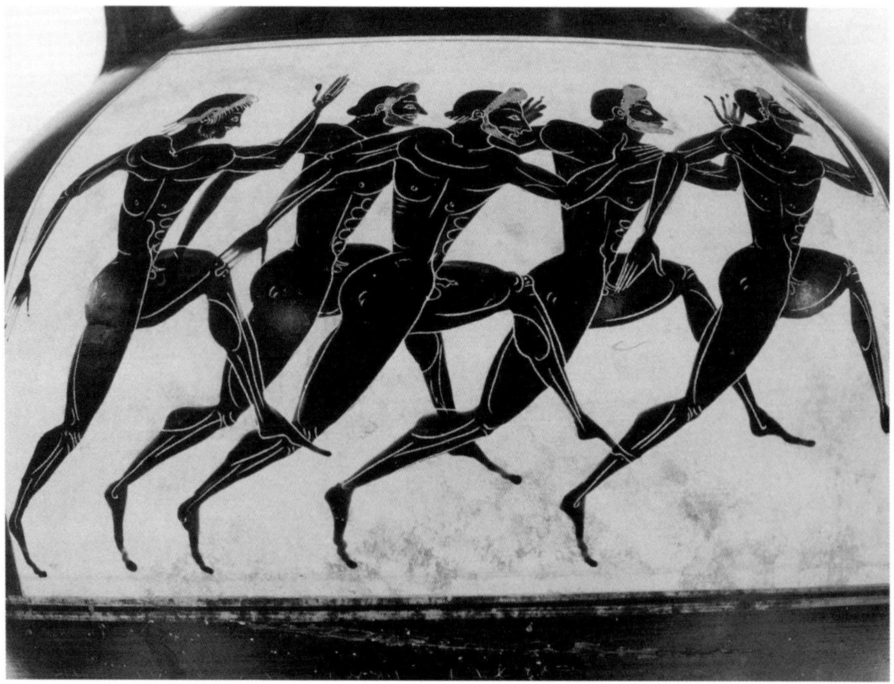

THE METROPOLITAN MUSEUM OF ART, ROGERS FUND, 1914

Figure 46. DETAIL OF A GREEK VASE, END OF VI CENT. B.C. ATHENIAN

spaced. (Each figure by itself has movement, but it is emphasized through this means.)

Let us now compare the detail of the Greek vase to Marcel Duchamp's "Nude Descending a Staircase" (*Figure 47*), done in 1912, 2500 years later than the vase. (In this work Duchamp combined the artistic aims of Cubism and Futurism.) This artist of the Futuristic movement (whose productive period was between 1910-1916) attempted to simultaneously depict a set of physical movements of a body as it is in reality.

In the Duchamp work we do visually experience movement. Even though there is an obviously vast difference in style from the Greek work (*Figure 46*), the same visual devices have been employed to produce the sense of visual movement. Duchamp, as we can see, has overlapped and repeated a number of basically similar forms. There is a difference in intention between the two works. The Greek artist (*Figure 46*) wished to represent five running figures while Duchamp (*Figure 47*) wished to represent a set of physical motions of a single human body walking down a staircase. One may further study and compare these two works. Every work of art possesses a degree of visual tension or movement which contributes to the unification of various forms in a work.

DIRECTION CAN UNIFY DIFFERENT AREAS OF A WORK OF ART

In the detail from El Greco's "The Adoration of the Shepherds" (*Figure 48*), we can see how the master used the principle of direction to unify different forms in the work. He uses the direction of the branch on the ground to unify the figure on our right with the figure whose foot appears on our left. In addition, the branch itself has direction and unifies the forms of the two figures by establishing cohesive forces between them. To our left there is a slight bend in the branch which is repeated in the shape or the form of the foot. At the other end, a forked branch is repeated in reverse by the triangular shape in the drapery of the figure. This is how El Greco produced the cohesive forces at the terminals of this branch, thereby connecting the forms of the figures, making them become part of the direction of the branch itself. We have therefore a series of cohesive forces, one produced by similarity of shape, at either end of the branch in conjunction with the similarity of direction. Such a device helps to forge the total pattern into one cohesive whole.

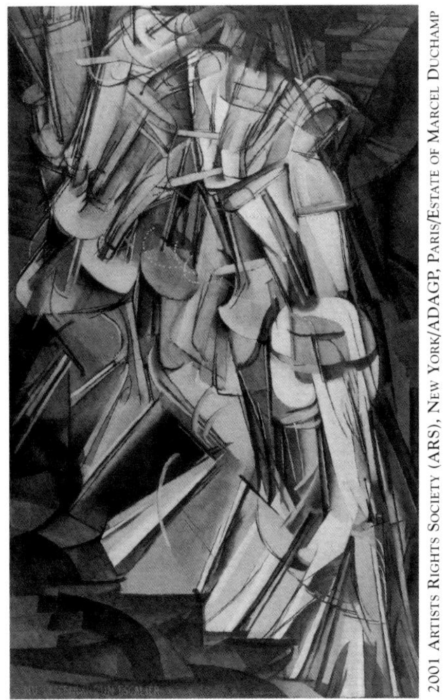

Figure 47. DUCHAMP, NUDE DESCENDING A STAIRCASE NO. 2, 1912

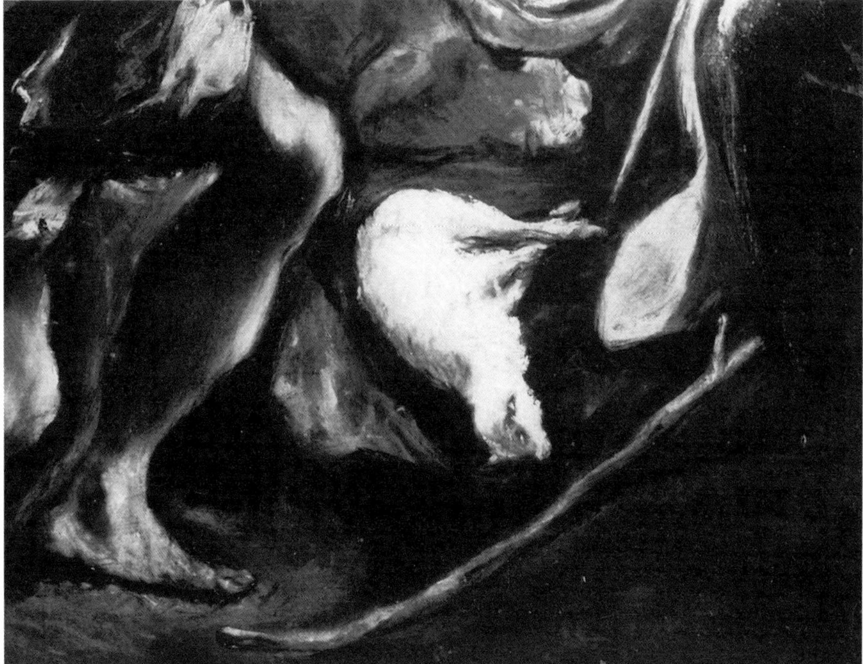

Figure 48. EL GRECO, THE ADORATION OF THE SHEPHERDS (Detail)

The Primacy of the Whole Structure of the Work of Art

In the section concerning the visual element of "Shape", we found that the major structural axis determines the dominant visual direction of the form. For example, in *Figure 4*, we see an isolated upright rectangle. The direction is a result of the strong verticality of the dominant axis. The brightness distribution (in *Figure 49*) creates a criss-cross pattern; that is, the dark rectangles form a simple cross while the light rectangles form an "X". The character of the individual structural axes has been preserved within the pattern. In *Figure 50*, however, we have a series of rectangles that have been arranged in a circular pattern, which has subordinated the individual or isolated character of the structural axis of the parts. These examples demonstrate how the nature of the whole structure of a work determines the individual character of the parts.

A fine example of what has been demonstrated (in *Figures 49* and *50*) is the detail from Albrecht Durer's "Expulsion from Paradise" (*Figure 51*) from the woodcut series "The Little Passion" which he did in 1510. If, starting from the top, we examine the directions of the various shapes on the left, the two heavy branches, the sword of the angel and the feathers of the angel's wings, we notice a gradual turning in space of the structural axes resulting in an arch-like shape for this section of the picture. Here the overall arrangement of the directions of the structural axes produces a dominant direction or visual movement that is different from what the direction of each part expresses in itself (*Figure 52*). Such overall directions or visual movement can be achieved also by the arrangements of color, brightness values or shapes. One can perform many exercises exploring and gaining control of this important means in achieving one's artistic aims.

The important factor of the primacy of overall structure of the work can be further clarified with the Kopfermann diagrams. It shows the direction of the framework tends to affect the forms which it encloses. For example, in *Figure 53*, the small form is experienced as a diamond within the larger rectangle. However in *Figure 54* the framework has been changed to an oblique direction. The smaller form maintains the same physical position. Yet its visual nature has been clearly affected. The small form now tends to be seen as a square rather than a diamond-like shape. The visual character of a form within a structure is not therefore determined by the isolated physical character, but by the visual nature of the whole structure.

Refer again to the Picasso collage (*Figure* 28) which has been executed with pasted-down pieces of newspaper, charcoal and ink. Looking at the work, we experience that the original function of the newspaper tends to be subordinated to its visual and expressive function within the inner structure of the whole work of art.

This has been accomplished by producing cohesive forces between the shapes of the pasted papers and the other forms in the work. This has been done by several means. The vertical direction of the line drawn in charcoal in the visual center of the work continues down the sides of the shapes of pasted paper. The base of the lower pasted paper has been cut into an arch whose visual direction is continued by the arch that has been drawn. This arch-like direction is repeated in various sections of the work, for instance, above it, which represents the shoulders of the man and the two arched lines above the two rectangles shapes of pasted papers. The shapes drawn within the two rectangular pasted papers (which represent the features of the man) are similar. We observe that the top horizontal line in the rectangular shape on the right continues beyond its boundaries, as it extends beyond the ear of the head which is formed by two lines drawn with the character of the number 3 which then becomes parallel to the horizontal line above it. The vertical line connected to it forms a right angle which is repeated and parallel to the visual right angle formed by the visually centered vertical line and the horizontal line described above which is tangent to the top of the form of the ear. The arrangement of forms create cohesive forces between the shapes of the pasted pieces of newspaper and the adjacent areas.

The diagonal lines within the two pasted rectangles are repeated in the larger diagonal line which begins at the form of the ear and continues downward until it meets the arch line. At this point the diagonal line is represented in reverse in the lower pasted paper, but both diagonal lines however point to a common visual destiny. Forms which have a common visual destiny tend to be unified. We have pointed out the major features which are responsible for producing cohesive forces between the shapes of the pasted papers and other shapes in the work. It is as in *Figure* 50 where the arrangement of shapes and brightness or color subordinated the individual character of the separate pieces by the nature of the whole structure which in the Picasso work minimizes or subordinates the original function of the pasted newspaper. This is another demonstration of the primary character of the overall structure of the work over its parts: a principle of the utmost importance to the understanding of the visual structure of a work of art.

The details from the fourth and eighth states of Rembrandt's etching "Ecce Homo" also demonstrate the priority of the structure over the character of the parts. In the fourth state (*Figure* 55) we have a squarish shape above the doorway and in between the two allegorical figures. In the eighth state (*Figure* 56) the squarish shape is still physically present, yet visually its importance has been altered. This has been produced by making different parts of the boundary of the shape function within a different pattern of visual forces. This has been done by several means: (1) The protrusion of the arch into the squarish shape and the darkening of the area enables the base of the square to have a more dominant visual function as part of the form of the doorway. (2) The shading of the right side reduces the visual effectiveness of the physical boundary of the square on that side. (3) Also the ten grayish forms on top minimize the visual importance of the physical boundary of the shape there. This kind of thing has been called the "hidden figure phenomenon" by Gottschaldt. We can see how this also applies to the discussion of the Picasso collage, where the original function of the newspaper as something to be read has been "hidden" within the more dominant structural forces of the work.

The Expressive Characteristics of Direction

In another detail from the Durer woodcut (*Figure* 57), we see that the juxtaposition of different and opposite directions in the criss-cross arrangement of the legs produces a certain degree of visual tension. This visual expression is emphasized by the stepping of Eve's foot on Adam's, an element understandable to us from past experience.

In Edvard Munch's lithograph "The Shriek" (*Figure* 58) done in 1895, the shriek emanating from the figure in the foreground is echoed

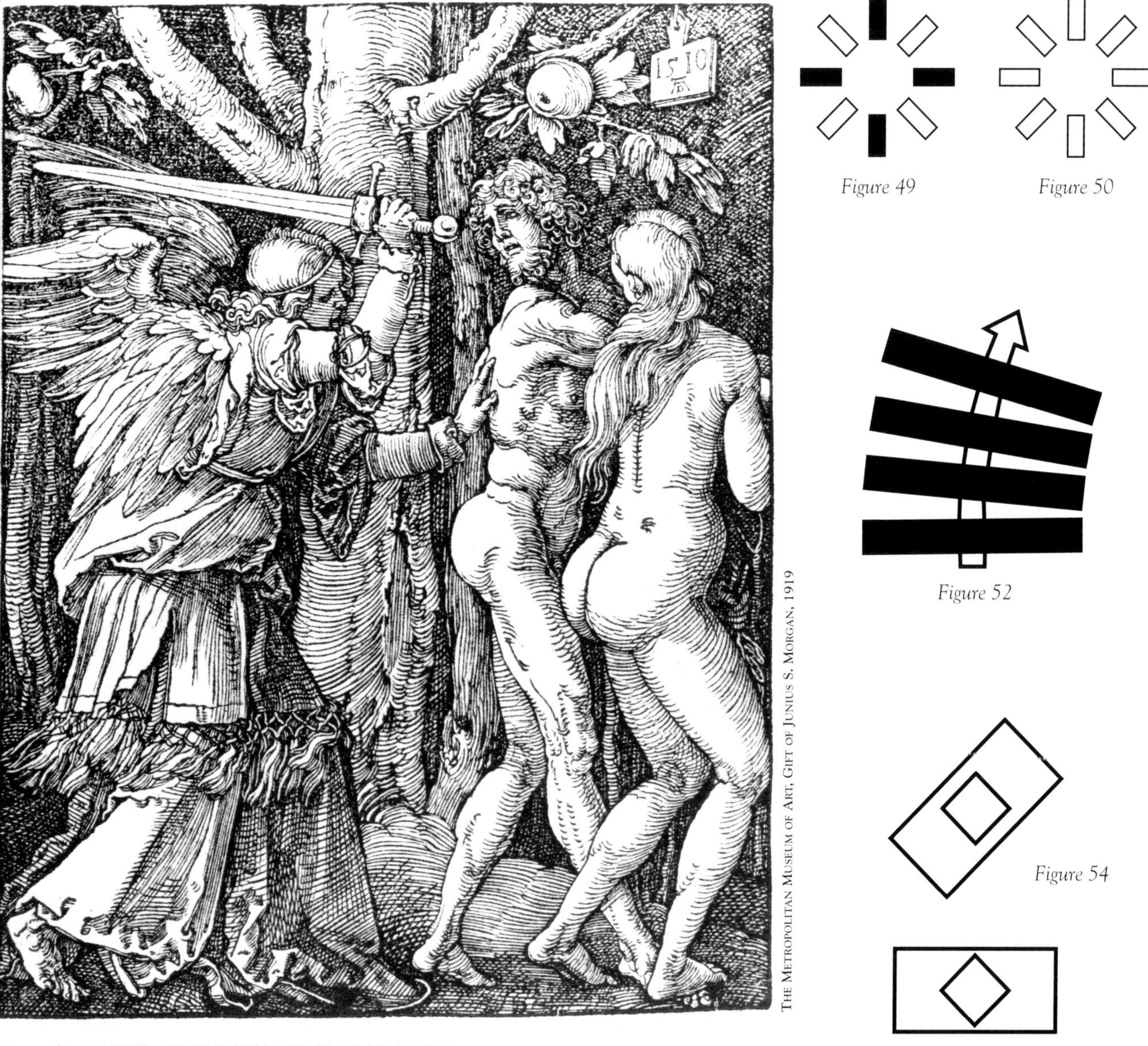

Figure 49

Figure 50

Figure 52

Figure 54

Figure 53

Figure 51. DURER, EXPULSION FROM PARADISE

THE METROPOLITAN MUSEUM OF ART, GIFT OF JUNIUS S. MORGAN, 1919

throughout the "Nature" setting around him. An analogy can be made with the physical effect that is created when we drop a pebble into a still water causing a series of concentric circles. This effect is most apparent in the shape of the mouth, the source of the cry which is complemented by the arrangement of lines within the skull-like head and hands that are holding it. The bulging eyeballs with their pinpoint pupils which are pointing in opposite directions (which parallel all the contrasting directions in the work) and in part create a frightful expression through a reference to our past experience. The rest of the work which basically repeats this expression, is derived from the nature of the visual structure. This creates a unity of expression throughout the work. The variety of visual direction, which has been unified, counteracts, counterpoints and complements each other to produce the visual tensions that help create the pure artistic expression of the work. These different and contrasting visual rhythms function within the boundaries of the work in a definite order which concentrates the intensity of expression. The general waviness of the lines throughout the print repeats the whirling form of the central figure. There is also a basic unity of the use of the bold character of lines which are generally arranged with alternating stripes of white between them. (An analogy can be made with a very bright light in a very dark room that flickers on and off.) Also, varying the space interval between the dark and white

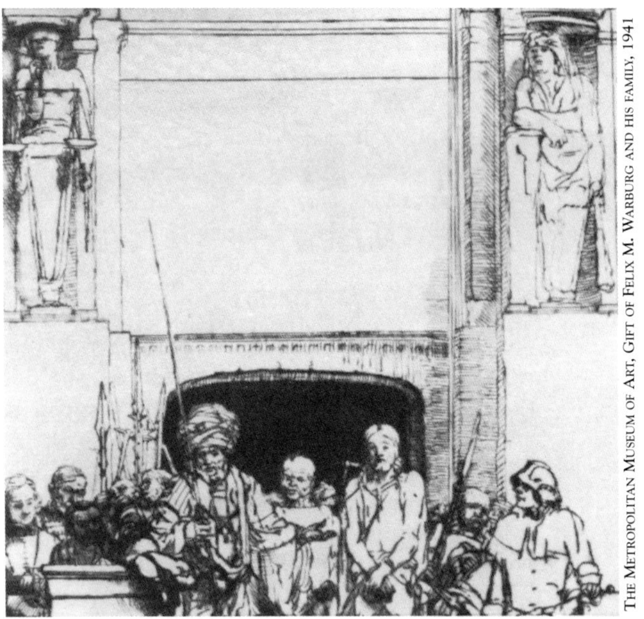

THE METROPOLITAN MUSEUM OF ART, GIFT OF FELIX M. WARBURG AND HIS FAMILY, 1941

Figure 55. REMBRANDT, CHRIST PRESENTED TO THE PEOPLE, STATE IV (Detail)

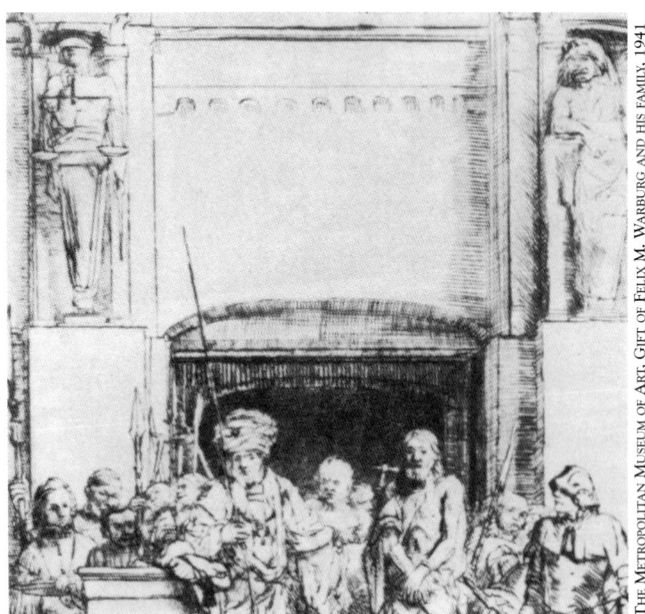

THE METROPOLITAN MUSEUM OF ART, GIFT OF FELIX M. WARBURG AND HIS FAMILY, 1941

Figure 56. REMBRANDT, CHRIST PRESENTED TO THE PEOPLE, STATE VIII (Detail)

areas produces a range of rhythms and intensity of expression.

We shall describe how these different directions have been generally unified within the whole work. At the right of the head, the triangular arrangement of a series of vertical and slightly wavy lines resemble sound waves whose apex falls within the area near the head. These vertical lines do not lead outside the picture space, but lead upward along the edge of the work into the sky. This upward visual movement is aided by the diagonal direction of the bold waving line at the top of this triangular pattern. The converging lines of the fence and road do not visually meet somewhere outside the picture space, but are visually "detoured" by the two dark figures at the "end" of the road. The curved directions of the lines on the road have a good continuation through the form of the figure at the edge of the work and up into the curves of the hills and the lines in the sky right above it. The unification of the different directions of the roadway and the sky is also aided by the general similarity of brightness produced by the similarity of the density of the lines. This visual movement is directed over the whole sky. The lines which make up the clouds in the sky flatten out as they reach the top of the work contributing to the retention of the visual direction within the picture space. The left side of it points downward towards the central figure. This is how Munch created a unified and dynamic "circular" pattern which functions throughout the picture.

The character of the form of the clouds in the sky wax and wane as do sound waves. The dynamic character of the visual directions have created strong visual tensions within the form, especially in the middle cloud which swells at one point. It is directed outward, and then it contracts where it is in a sense "pinched" with greater visual tension imposed on it from the white area outside it at that point. One can discover other instances of how Munch employed this kind of counterbalancing directions or visual tensions in other areas to produce the particular dramatic expression of the work.

PRE-OUTLINED EXERCISES 7-17 (SHEETS 2 AND 3)

The general purpose of exercises 7-17 is to present one kind of approach by which the student can gain some experience in controlling the use of the visual elements in producing desired patterns of forms. These exercises are presented in three different arrangements of shapes: (A) 7-9, (B) 10-13 and (C) 14-17. The basic task that the student is to perform is to make different patterns by varying the arrangement of brightness and color qualities, within the same arrangement of shapes in each group, using the standard set of tempera colors of red, yellow, blue, green, black

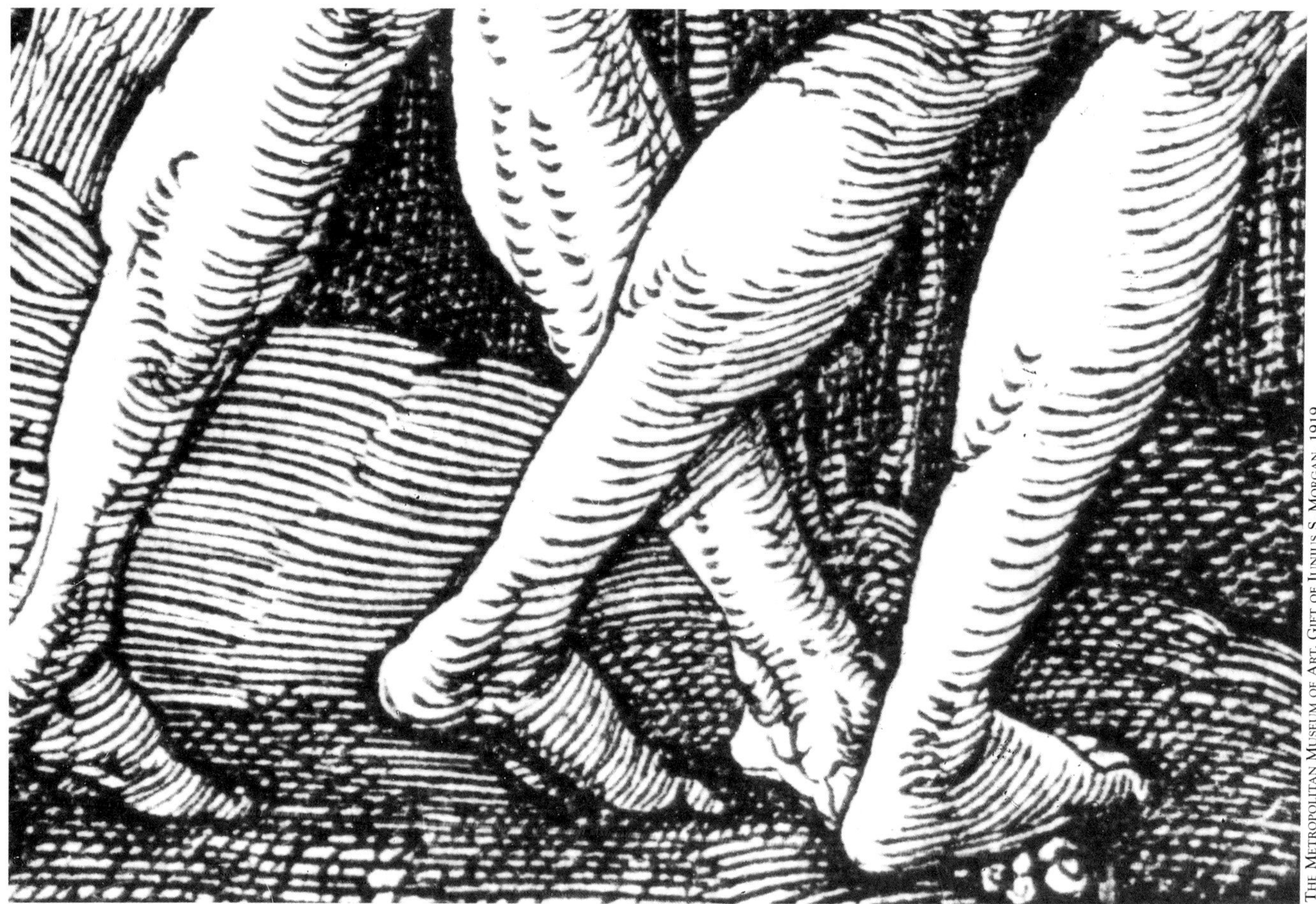

Figure 57. DURER, EXPULSION FROM PARADISE (*Detail*)

and white. The colors can be used pure or intermixed. After these exercises have been completed the student can if he wishes do supplementary exercises by using blank sheets and varying the characteristics and arrangements of shapes. Maintain the same general similar structural quality through the use of brightness and color between the different treatments and arrangements of shapes. Also experiment with arrangement of forms having similar or dissimilar textures produced by different means.

The Factor of Closure

The factor of closure completes perceptually that which is physically incomplete. This is due to the cohesive forces produced by the form. Closure is considered as a logical extension of the factor of direction. For example, the form of a circle, square or triangle, that is not completely drawn is experienced nevertheless as a complete form, rather than scattered and unrelated lines (*Figure 59*). Closure has been used by many artists. In art, closure should not be left to accident, it must be produced intentionally by the artist and it in time will become automatic. Often certain indications or arrangements of form enhance the experiencing of closure.

In *Figure 60*, we visually experience two circles and one half circle on either side of them. This effect can be diminished by changing the two halves of the circles to different brightness and colors. In *Figure 61* we have changed the orientation of the same parts so that the half circles do not visually continue into the other, producing segregating forces between them and creating three different visual units of "X's". In *Figure 62* the distances between the half circles has been increased, producing greater segregating forces between the half circles and diminishing the effect of closure. Due to the factor of nearness of the half circles, which are back to back, we again tend to experience three different visual units of "X's".

We have reproduced two drawings of similar houses of the low lands, one by Pieter Bruegel the

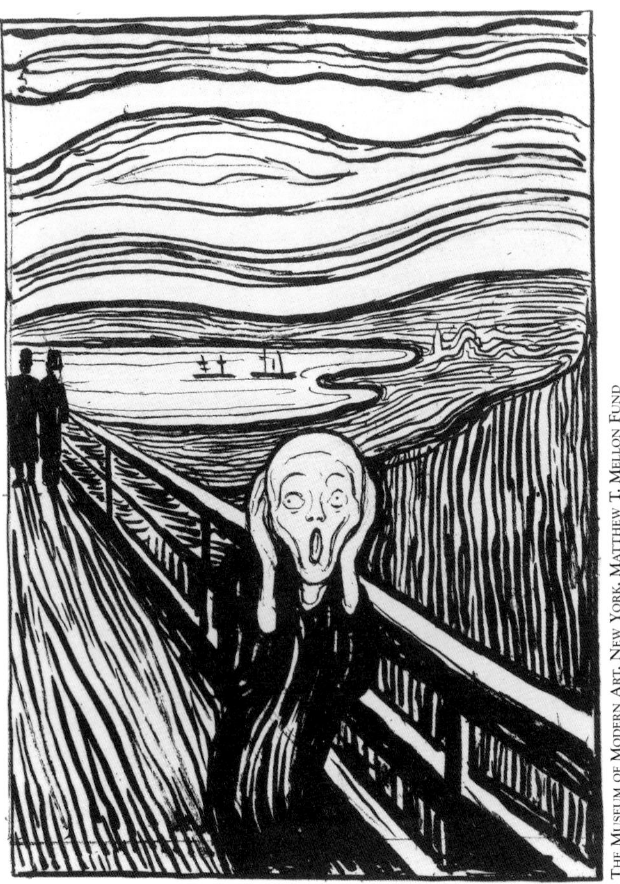

Figure 58. EDVARD MUNCH, THE SHRIEK (1896, Lithograph, printed in black, composition, 13 15/16" x 10")

The Museum of Modern Art, New York. Matthew T. Mellon Fund

Elder (*Figure* 63) and the other by Rembrandt (*Figure* 64.) We can obviously see the vast differences in approach to the same subject matter. The Bruegel drawing more fully records the physical nature of the houses as they appeared in reality, than Rembrandt's treatment which is more sketchy and utilizes the factor of closure. The use of closure presents the artists with another means to create artistic forms. Kurt Koffka (1935) has indicated that closure produces greater perceptual work. In other words: an incomplete circle has greater visual tension than a complete circle.

Another example of closure is Degas' oil sketch (*Figure* 65). The skirt of the ballet dancer to our left is not completely indicated, yet we experience it as complete. The skirt of the dancer on our right is fully represented and lies in the same position and direction as the incomplete one. This parallel arrangement contributes to the creation of closure. The hem of the dress on the left is partially indicated. This is one of the several major features used by Degas to create closure. Also in both figures the drawing of the legs protrudes into the area of the dress. The freely brushed on color that lies in a general vertical direction, visually connects the top of the dress to the legs. This establishes a visual connection or unity between the torso and the legs. Our main finding is that Degas rendered the two skirts by two different visual means: (1) through closure, and (2) complete representation of the form, and that he obtained basically the same visual result. Yet these differences produced variety. To use a simpler example: we could have a circle completely rendered and another circle not completely rendered, but completed by closure. We would obtain perceptual completeness in both of them which produces a structural similarity, and therefore unity, and from their physical differences we would also experience variety.

Hard and Soft Colors

We have seen in a preceding section that cohesive forces can be produced through a similarity of colors and brightness. Kurt Koffka and M. R. Harrower have discovered an important property of color which has a great bearing on the creation of unity within variety in a work of art. They have found that different colors and brightnesses can be generally classified in terms of visual "hardness" and "softness." Red, yellow and white are visually hard, while blue, green and black are visually soft. As regards the effects on unity and variety, hard colors tend to produce segregating forces while soft colors tend to be unified or produce cohesive forces between themselves.

As we shall see, the effect of hard and soft colors can be controlled by the nature of shape and brightness, making us more aware of the very important principle that the different visual elements must not be thought of as isolated or unrelated. The pre-outlined exercises 18-24 will enable us to more clearly understand the influence of the nature of the visual elements upon each other in the creation of the visual structure.

Pre-outlined Exercises 18-24 (Sheets 4 and 5)

To demonstrate the basic nature of hard and soft colors, complete the series of pre-outlined exercises which are made of checkerboard patterns 18-20.

(1) In Exercise 18, using tempera colors, create a pattern that has an approximate or equal amount of squares of red and yellow which are hard colors.

(2) In Exercise 19, still maintaining the same pattern in Exercise 18, substitute, for example, the soft colors blue and green.

(3) In Exercise 20, still maintaining the same pattern where you painted in blue in Exercise 19, substitute red for blue and repeat the exact arrangement of green.

Results: The student will find that in Exercise 18, there is a higher degree of variety with the arrangement of the hard colors, than in Exercise 19 which employ only soft colors. In Exercise 20, the structure produced tends to create less extreme degrees of unity or variety because of the combination of hard and soft colors within a single pattern.

Hard and Soft Colors and Brightness

Using the programmed Exercises 21-22 of this series, one can explore what the effect of changes in brightness of hard and soft colors have on the degree of unity and variety.

(4) Maintaining the same colors and arrangement in Exercise 18, begin by repeating the arrangement of yellow in the checkerboard pattern. Then apply a pale red (a red lightened with white.) This change of brightness in the red will increase the cohesive forces between the two colors, and reduce the original degree of variety in Exercise 18, because of the natural darkness of a saturated red is now lightened to approximate the natural lightness of a saturated yellow. It is this similarity of brightness that has increased the degree of unity.

(5) Exercise 22: Maintain the same arrangement of blue and green as in Exercise 19, but change the brightness of the colors. Significantly lighten, for example, the blue with white, and then darken the green with black. This difference in brightness created by the addition of black and white to the colors has increased the segregating forces or degree of variety.

Influence of Hard and Soft Colors on Form

As we have seen (Structure Section), different structures can be ambiguous and unambiguous. This is the case in Exercises 23 and 24. In Exercise 23 the structure can be seen either as two V's or one W. These exercises shall demonstrate the effect that hard and soft colors have on the formation of the visual character of the form.

(6) Exercises 23 and 24: Paint in the colors as they are indicated in the exercise. In Exercise 23 the colors are "hard" while in Exercise 24, they are "soft".

Results: In Exercise 23 the structure will tend to appear as two distinct V's while in Exercise 24 they will tend to appear as "fused" into a W. The ambiguity that existed before the colors were added has been greatly diminished.

In Exercise 23 the W is subordinate to the V while in Exercise 24 the V is subordinate to the W. As we have seen the squarish shape was embedded in the detail from Rembrandt's "Ecce Homo" (*Figure 55 and 56*).

We can see then, that segregating forces tend to emphasize the visual nature of the individual forms in the structure while cohesive forces tend to subdue their visual distinctness resulting in a greater overall unity of the different areas of the structure.

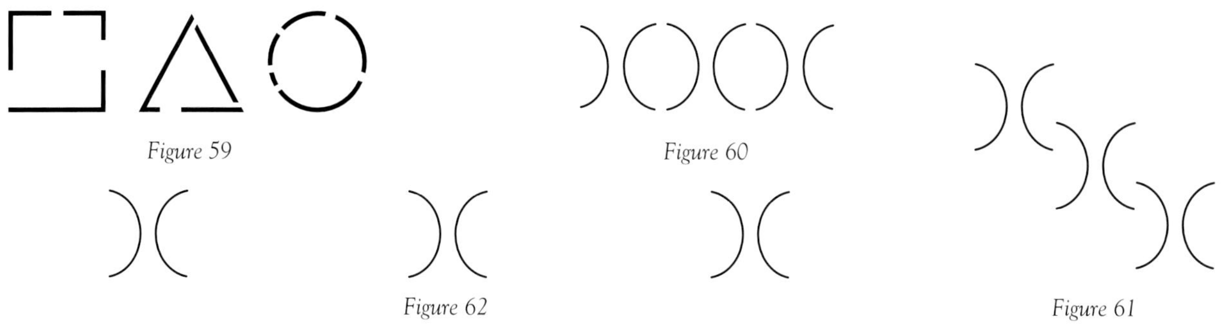

Figure 59

Figure 60

Figure 62

Figure 61

Cohesive and Segregating Forces and the Tendency Towards Simplicity

To further understand the nature of structural forces, we must take into consideration the fact that cohesive and segregating forces always tend toward the simplest possible arrangement available in the picture plane. This principle has been clearly illustrated in the writings of Rudolf Arnheim.

In *Figure* 66, we have four separate units which are placed in a particular arrangement, but they are seen as a single whole, rather than four separate parts, for the cohesive forces have organized them into one simple visual unit. This is similar to what occurs in the factors of similarity, nearness, direction and closure. *Figure 67* is seen as a rectangle and a circle, rather than a single complex form. A combination of the segregating and cohesive forces determines the simplicity of the form. The segregating forces separate the circle from the rectangle, whereas

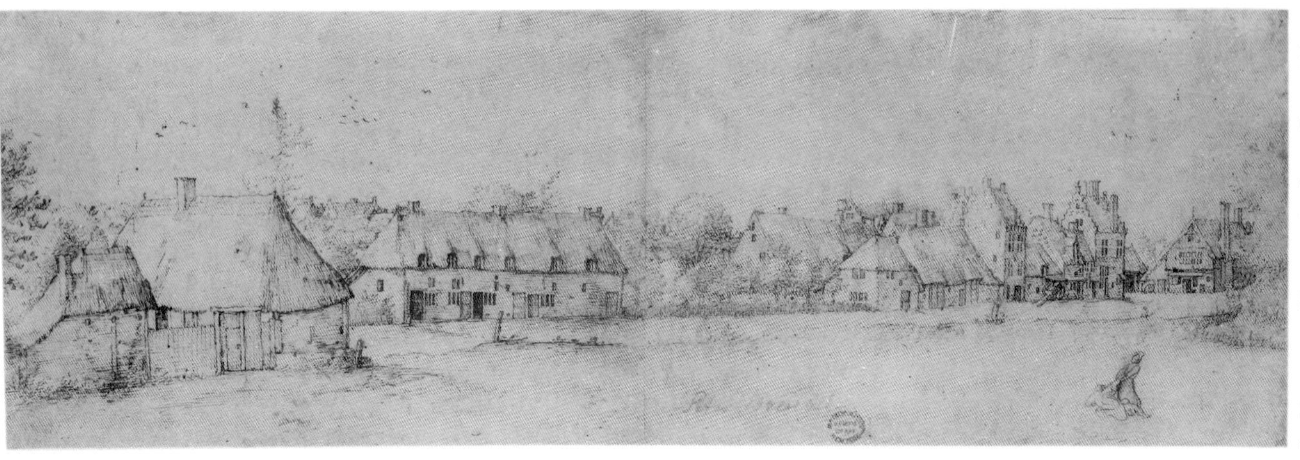

Figure 63. PIETER BRUEGEL THE ELDER, STREET SCENE IN A VILLAGE

The Metropolitan Museum of Art, Rogers Fund, 1906

Figure 64. REMBRANDT, HOUSES BY THE WATER

The Metropolitan Museum of Art, The H.O. Havemeyer Collection, Bequest of Mrs. H.O. Havemeyer, 1929

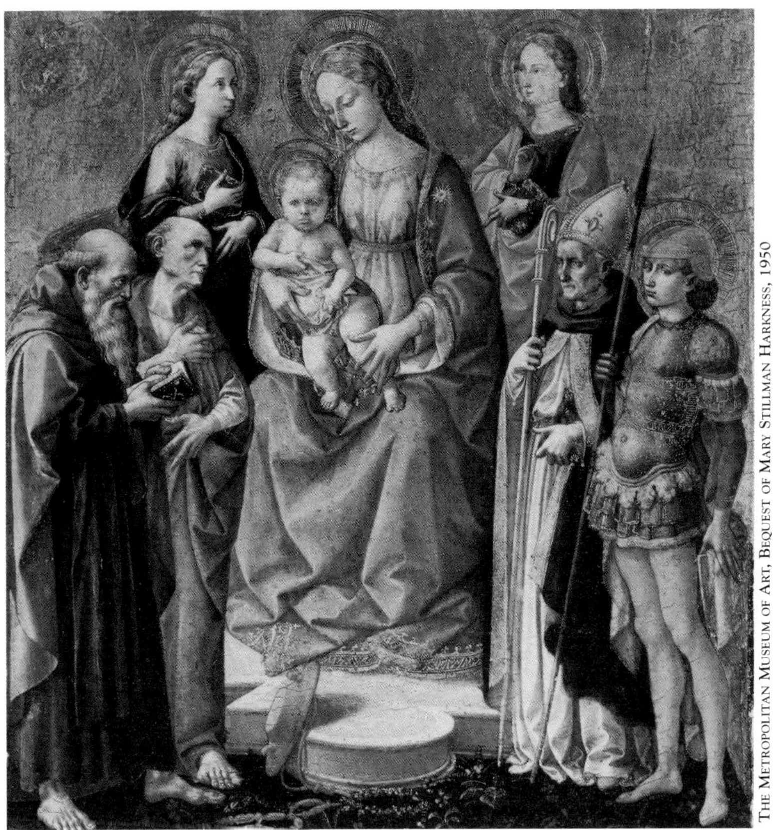

The Metropolitan Museum of Art, Bequest of Mary Stillman Harkness, 1950

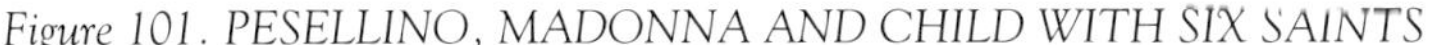

Figure 101. PESELLINO, MADONNA AND CHILD WITH SIX SAINTS

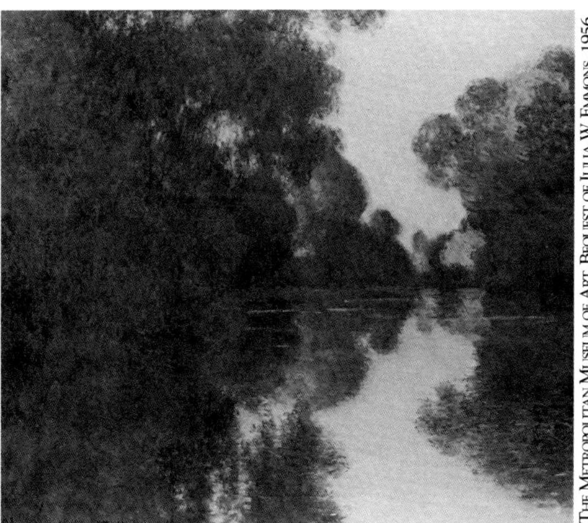

The Metropolitan Museum of Art, Bequest of Julia W. Emmons, 1956

Figure 102. MONET, MORNING ON THE SEINE NEAR GIVERNY

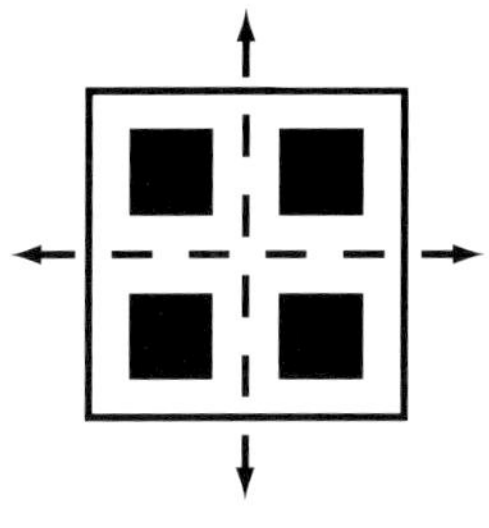

Figure 100

art have been created within many different kinds of boundaries. For example, "The Flight Into Egypt" by Cosimo Tura (*Figure 105*) is painted within a circle. The circular boundary influences particular organization of the work. We will in this section describe the factor of visual counterpointing within a rectangular boundary which has been more generally used, but the principles described will have a universal application to all kinds of boundaries.

(A) In *Figure 108*, with a series of four straight lines, we have indicated the major features of the structural map of the rectangle, representing the absolute minimum degree of counterpointing which is a completely complementary pattern of the symmetrical structural map. In *Figure 109*, we have two rectangular shapes parallel to and enclosed by the boundaries. This symmetrical arrangement is another form of a minimum degree of counterpointing the structural map. For it does not disturb, but fits within the main lines of the structural map.

(B) In the painting by Jacques Villon, "Abstraction" done in 1923 (*Figure 110*), we observe that it combines features represented in *Figures 108 and 109*, i.e., lines emanating from the "corners" and the rectangular shape in center is parallel to the boundaries of the work. If the diagonal lines were continued they would meet and form an "X" to completely indicate this feature of the structural map. This was not done. The diagonal features of the structural map of the smaller rectangle is the visual rather than a physical continuation of it. Villon did not in his arrangement of brightness and color exactly complement the symmetrical character of the structural map.

Villon then superimposed over this visually symmetrical arrangement a winding line. One can see a line of a baroque character which has been superimposed over a classic symmetrical arrangement of forms, thus creating a clear counterpoint with the structural map and the almost visual equivalent of it that was rendered by the artist. The circular part of the winding line as we observe is off center and is contrasted with the rectangular shape underneath it in the visual space.

"The Cup" done in 1917-18 by Georges Braque (*Figure 111*) is another example of the

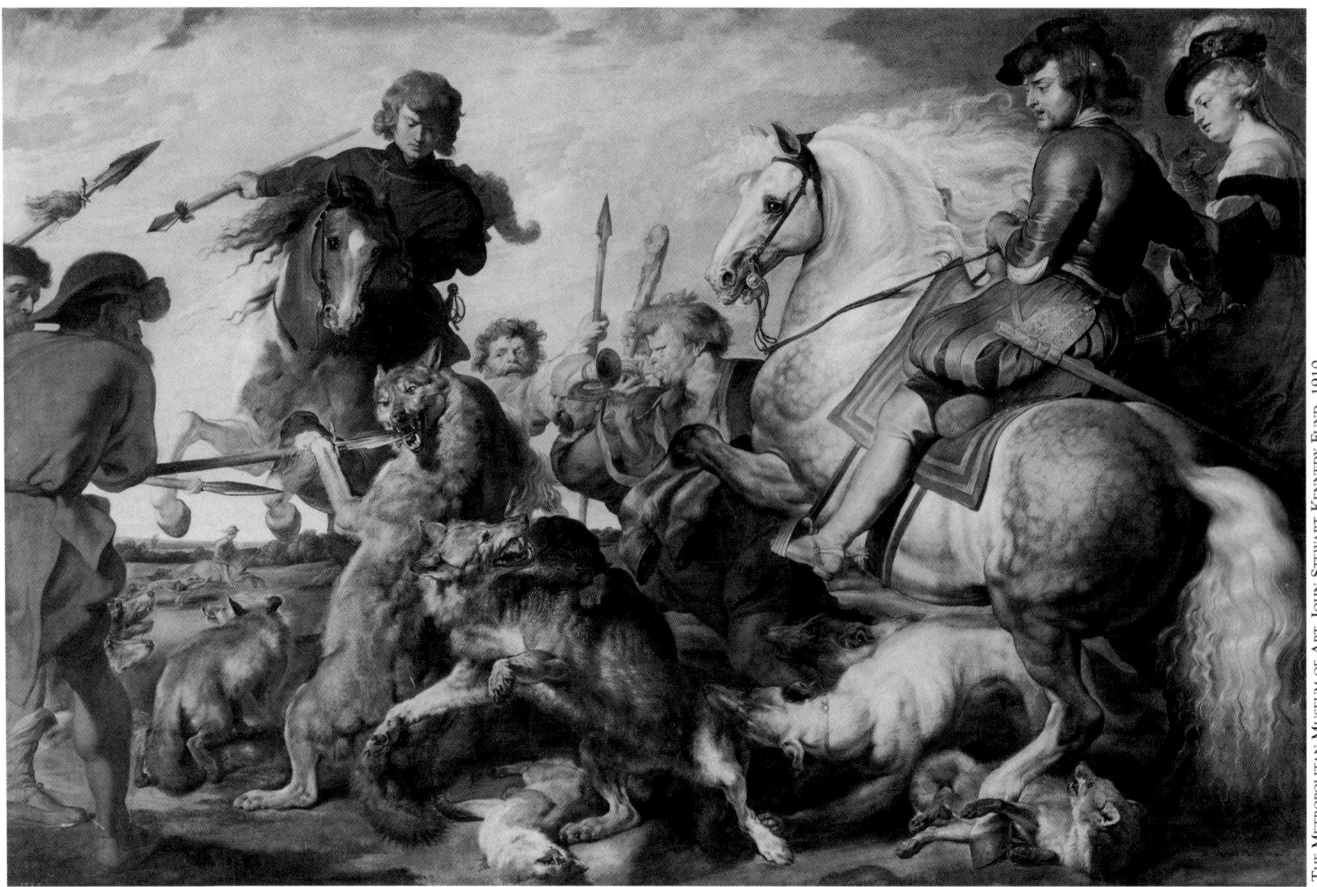

Figure 103. PETER PAUL RUBENS, WOLF AND FOX HUNT

structural map being indicated linearly and then counterpointed by the asymmetrical arrangement of brightness and color and placement of other forms. This is also an example of how different patterns formed by brightness, color and shape can counterpoint each other. The diagonal lines that indicate the structural map do not exactly terminate at the corners which subtly counterpoints the structural map.

(C) In Piet Mondrian's "Composition in Black and Gray" done in 1919 (*Figure 112*), we have a clear example of how the artist consciously avoided an emphasis of the main lines of visual force in the structural map. In this work, we see that the squarish shape of the boundaries of the work, has been orientated as a diamond-like framework which does not change the nature of the structural map, but only its directional aspects.

The work is basically divided into a checkerboard pattern of thin lines. Each of the 64 squares that have been formed has been divided into four triangles by means of horizontal and vertical lines. The resulting *Figure 113* can visually produce countless structural possibilities can emerge (refer to the structure section on ambiguous structures) through different emphasis of selected lengths of lines. One can explore some of the basic structural possibilities that can be developed (or other similar patterns) by changing the emphasis on certain linear aspects of the pattern and through different arrangements of color and brightness.

In *Figure 114*, we have indicated the arrangement of all the darkened horizontal lines and in *Figure 115*, all the darkened vertical lines. *Figure 114* demonstrates that the horizontal lines are generally longer and closer together the further away they are from the horizontal axis of the structural map. This also holds true for the arrangement of the vertical lines (*Figure 115*).

We see that there is no dominant correspondence between the vertical and horizontal patterns of rectangles formed by the arrangement of lines with the main axes of the structural map. We observe also that the top and bottom of the work have strong horizontal lines that

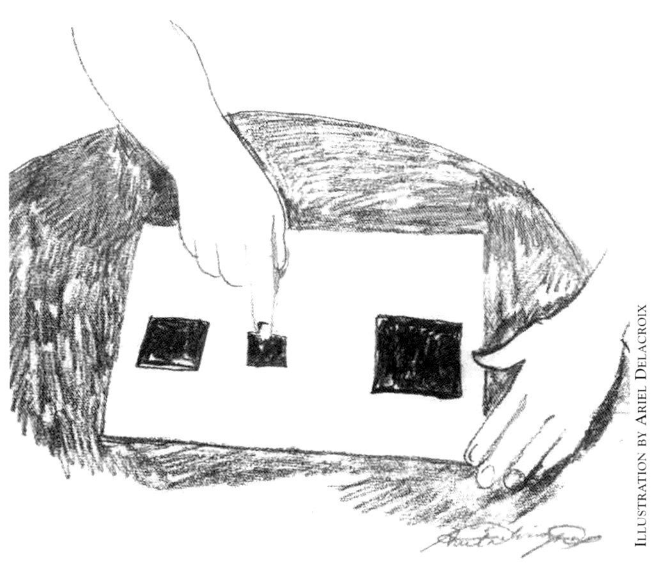

ILLUSTRATION BY ARIEL DELACROIX

Figure 104

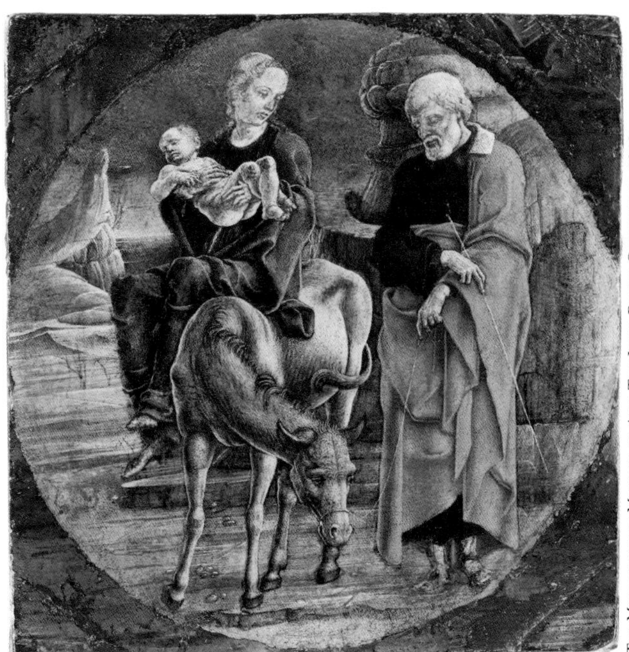

THE METROPOLITAN MUSEUM OF ART, THE JULES BACHE COLLECTION, 1949

Figure 105. COSIMO TURA, THE FLIGHT INTO EGYPT

"cut" across the corners contributing to a counteracting of the vertical axis of the structural map. The top was cut closer to the corner than the other three. At the bottom and left, the corners were closed by one bold stroke. This is not true in the right hand corner with its straight vertical that does not completely cut the area. It is interesting to note that in the top and bottom corners the vertical line down the center does not go completely to the edge. This is also true in the right hand corner where the horizontal does not meet the edge of the corner. We also notice in this work that the pattern formed by the dark lines has been superimposed over the pattern formed by the different designs and arrangements of thin lines which contribute to the variety of the work.

Our analysis of Mondrian's "Composition in Black and Gray" shows us how even down to the smallest detail this modern master clearly avoided any great emphasis of the dominant axes of the structural map. This again demonstrates how artists are completely aware of the structural map and take it into consideration in the creation of their works.

Counterpointing the Structural Map

In this section we shall consider a special form of visual counterpointing. Our analysis of the Villon, Braque and Mondrian works reveal a form of counterpointing that physically indicates on the canvas some or most of the features of the structural map.

We have now come upon the kind of counterpointing where there is no physical indication of the structural map, but takes it into definite consideration. In another work (*Figure 116*) by Piet Mondrian "Painting I" done in 1926, is an example of a pattern that clearly counterpoints the structural map. This has been accomplished within a diamond shape boundary of the work which is counterpointed by a visually square form that has been created by the factor of closure. We can see that three of the visual corners of the square form are outside the boundaries of the work. This has a stronger counterpointing effect than in the arrangement shown in *Figure 117* where we have the diamond framework completely enclosing the squarish pattern or form.

The two thickest black lines at the bottom and right side of the visual square which carries greater visual weight, aid in "closing" the visual square while the thinner lines that are reserved for the top left hand corner of the square are completely physically rendered. It is important to notice that it is not a true corner of a square, but that the vertical and horizontal lines visually continue outside the visual boundaries of the work. We see that the use of the surrounding space outside the work is not accidental or haphazard. It is incorporated and unified within the whole structure of the work.

The utilization of the factor of closure and the dynamic situation that incorporates the visual space outside the physical boundaries of the work make this seemingly simple work, a very dynamic one where every portion functions actively in the shaping of the effect of the whole structure of the work. There are no visually dead areas which is an important requirement of a work of art. Unity in this work has been achieved by the similarity of the boundaries of the diamond-like framework and the visually square form. Variety has been achieved through the difference in orientation of the shapes which produce different dominant visual directions for the axes. It is the difference in these axes that has created the counterpoint within a visually symmetrical work.

Paul Cezanne's painting, "The Large Bathers" (*Figure 118*), is a symmetrically balanced work and a subject which the master treated numerous times. The axes of the forms of the figures on either side of the work parallel and repeat the direction of the trees creating a structural map produced by the rectangular boundaries of the work. This Cezanne work is another basic example of the kind of visual counterpoint found in Piet Mondrian's "Painting I" (*Figure 116*).

Full Visual Counterpoint

Full visual counterpoint is present in a work of art when the visual directions of the forms or patterns counterpoint each other, and, when they in turn are so arranged as to counterpoint the whole structural map. "Wolf and Fox Hunt" by Peter Paul Rubens (*Figure 103*) is a fine example of full visual counterpoint, as are many other Baroque works. We can observe a dominant visual movement from the right, which is counterpointed (or counteracted) by the diagonal directions of several forms on the left. An example is the horseman and the figure holding the spear, battling with the wolf standing on its hind legs. The visual direction of the wolf is also diagonal and is counterpointed by the opposing direction of the wolf next to him. The character of the counterpointing of the two wolves is representative of, or repeats, the character of the dominant counterpointing directions of the work.

We have in this section described the major factors of structural hierarchy. We can never view a work of art as a visually still surface or flat surface. The dynamic visual forces of a work function throughout the entire picture space at different depth levels and the intervals between them.

Hierarchy of Expression

In the preceding sections we have stated the importance of unity within variety and balance in a work of art. Here, a disturbing question arises. It is self-evident that in art, literature and music for example, there have been expressions of confusion, instability and monotony which the principles of unity within variety and balance are supposed to avoid. Artists have described, for example, the monotony of prison life, the confusion of a retreat in battle, or the instability of a mentally disturbed person. There are other disturbing expressions directly derived from the structure, such as the agitation derived from the structure of the details of the Van Eyck (*Figure 25*) and the Van Gogh (*Figure 24*) works discussed earlier in this study.

The problem then is how can unpleasant expressions exist simultaneously in a stable and pleasurable framework. The answer to this important question can lead to a deeper understanding of the general nature of expression and form in art.

As we have previously seen, pure artistic expression is derived from the nature of the structure. Structure and expression are two inseparable concepts. It was also demonstrated in *Figures 12-13* in terms of structure, that the isolated parts do not determine the nature of the structure. This concept equally holds true for pure artistic expression. For example, we can have a musical phrase that in itself may be pleasing. As we know, if the phrase were repeated indefinitely a monotonous expression would eventually result. This monotony is a result of the whole structure of our

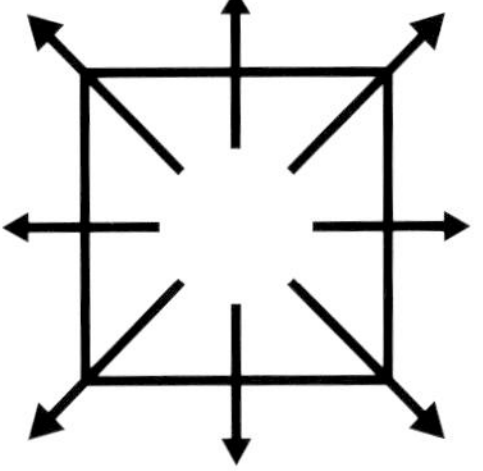

Figure 106

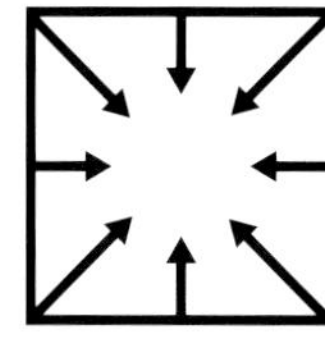

Figure 107

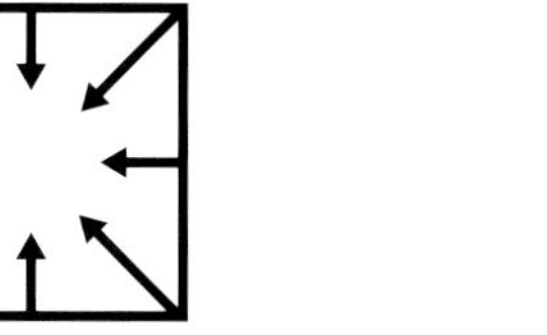

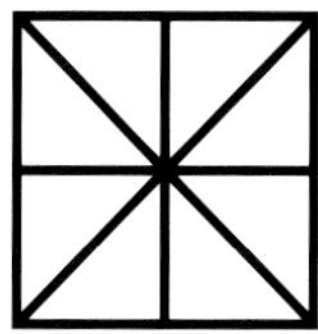

Figure 108

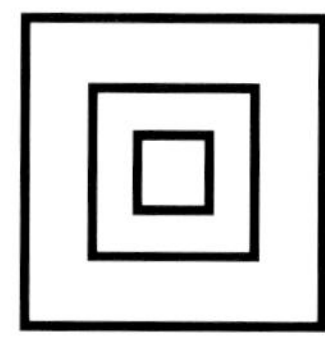

Figure 109

experience of all the repetitions rather than experiencing the isolated or separated musical phrases themselves. Therefore, the nature of the whole special structure of a work of art is the primary influence on the nature of the meaning and expression. This is an important concept for understanding the nature of expression of a work of art.

Stravinsky, the famous contemporary composer, stated that the expression in music (or a work of art) is different from the expression or meaning found in reality. A very clear example of this distinction of expression between art and reality can be seen by comparing in our minds the detail from the Durer work (*Figure 119*) representing a group of figures being trampled beneath the hooves of the four horses, with how we would experience the same event while walking down the street. Our reaction would of course, be quite different from that derived from a work of art. From this self-evident comparison we become clearly aware of the basically different attitudes, even with the same basic event, we tend to have toward a work of art and reality.

We shall show how the unpleasant expression is fused within a stable and pleasurable framework of a visual work of art. In *Figure 119*, a detail from Albrecht Durer's woodcut, "The Riders on the Four Horse from the Apocalypse", done in 1498, a group of human figures are so arranged that on a short exposure for a second or two, an expression of confusion or disorder will tend to be experienced. This expression can be directly traced to purely visual features. We observe that the facial expressions can be understood by our past experience or knowledge as expressions of despair, confusion, etc., but more essentially the intensity of the expression of "confusion" is embedded in the juxtaposition of different directions of the structural axes of the forms (*Figure 120*) represented by the arrangement of the structural axes in this section of the woodcut. By isolating just this one structural feature, we have still retained the basic expression of "confusion." We can therefore say, that the greater part of the expression of "confusion" is produced purely by the visual tensions that are embedded in the variety and opposing directions of the structural axes.

If we begin to analyze this detail carefully, we will discover that the opposition of different directions of structural axes has actually a dual expressive function. It creates the expression of confusion, and also serves in part to counterbalance the different directions assuring stability or balance. The same structural feature possesses opposite expressions, one pleasant and the other unpleasant which demonstrates the hierarchy of pure artistic expression. The expression of balance or stability has been subdued, or subordinated, to the expression of confusion. We can observe a similar situation in the Munch work (*Figure 58*).

For example, the head of the man which is sticking out slightly above and to our left of the head of the heavy man lying on the floor is in direct opposition to the visual direction of the heavy man's head, and also the forearm of the standing man. In terms of reality it may seem strange for the head to be just sticking up or almost pasted right next to the head of the heavy man, but this was done in order to achieve a counterbalance. So the placement of this head was apparently motivated by the dual wish to counterbalance this direction and to add another opposing direction which would add to the expression of confusion. Similarly, we notice a fallen clergyman at the extreme right hand corner, with his face down on the ground. Its visual direction is in direct opposition to the calf of the standing man. The reader will discover for himself other instances of the opposing and counterbalancing

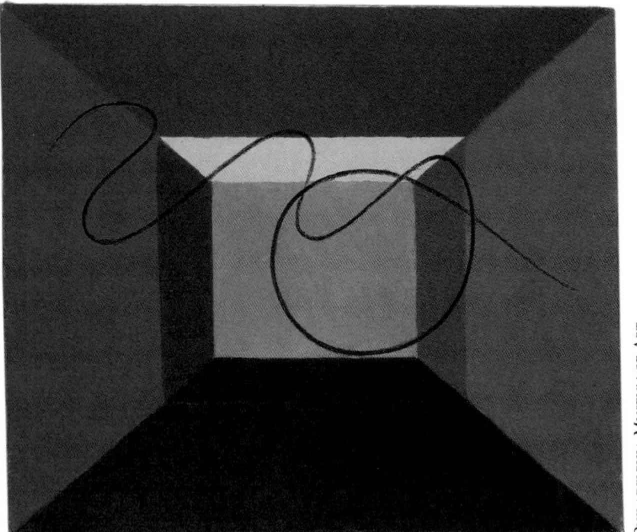

Philadelphia Museum of Art, The Louise and Walter Arensberg Collection

Figure 110. VILLON, ABSTRACTION, 1932

visual direction and the general patterns or artistic order in this detail. Also it is important to observe that this particular section (*Figure 119*) is counterbalanced and is unified with other sections of the work (*Figure 121*).

The confusion we experience from the disorganized or excessive variations of visual elements is the expression of confusion itself. In the Durer work the expression of confusion is experienced within an organized framework. The presentation of any pleasurable or unpleasant expression within a stable, pleasurable framework is one of the main determinants of a work of art. We have demonstrated through the Durer example that the expression of a work of art is not of the same nature that we may derive from an ordinary experience.

There are two important factors which we shall consider that contribute to the expression or meaning of a form in a work of art. (A) The nature and character of the visual properties of the form itself; and if it is a realistic form, its specific reference to our past experience and knowledge. We will call this factor the original expression, which in special cases supplies a general index of the form's expression in a work of art. (B) The second factor and the most important is how the expression of the form is influenced by it's arrangement within the overall structure of the work. This factor can affect the visual appearance of the form, and therefore affects

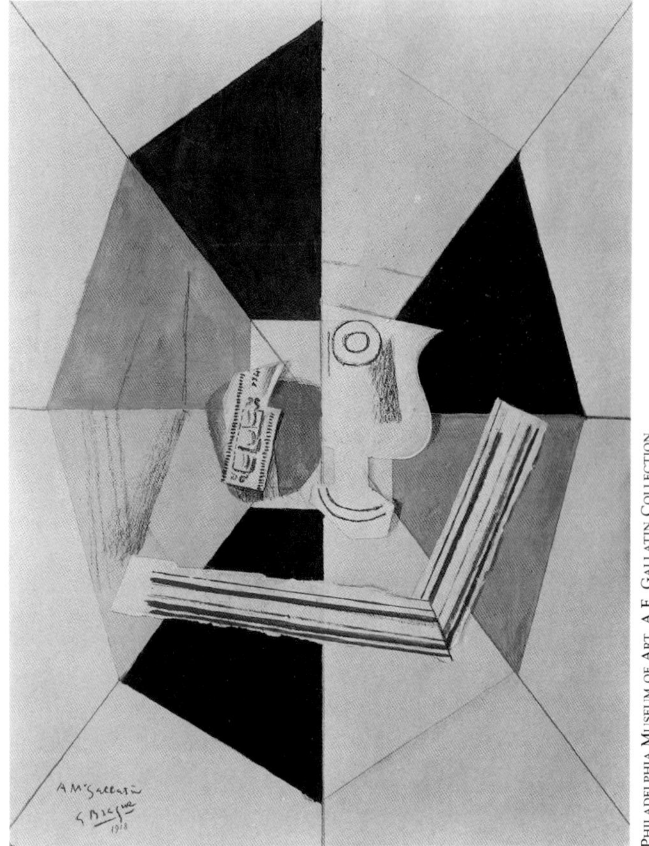

Philadelphia Museum of Art, A.E. Gallatin Collection

Figure 111. GEORGES BRAQUE, THE CUP

its expression. This holds true for both realistic and pure visual forms. This factor has the significant role in giving a form in a work its particular expressive identity.

One of the important results of the analysis of the Durer detail (*Figure 119*) is that we found that expressions which are generally similar can be critically different in terms of the world of art, produced by the nature and character of the framework it exists in. Keeping this principle in mind, let us take the case of an identical form which is represented in different works; and, for example, in each instance it is visually isolated and not strongly unified with other sections of the structure, thereby the original visual and expressive character of the form tends to be generally preserved. However, since the framework differs in each work, the expression of the form in each case will have a different expressive identity. Therefore, we observe that there is no fixed expressive identity assigned to a form under varying conditions or frameworks.

The original expression of a form can be subdued to different degrees or almost completely "hidden" by making it function as part of a larger pattern whose dominant expression may be entirely different. On page 24 of this book we observed from details of Rembrandt's etching (*Figure* 55) how the squarish form was "hidden" in a later state (*Figure* 56) thereby creating an entirely different visual and expressive effect. On pages 20-22 we described how Picasso (*Figure 28*) subdued the original expression or meaning of the pieces of newspaper in the collage. (The original function and meaning of a newspaper is determined by our past experience and knowledge.) What happened in essence in the Picasso work is that the original meaning or function of the newspaper was subordinated to its purely visual properties and the expression it produces.

We have seen that the same shape, brightness and color of a pure visual or representational form with the same original reference to our past experience and knowledge can be changed to produce or contribute to a wide range of structural and expressive qualities.

We can conclude on the basis of the above discussion that: Every work of art is a completely unique structural and expressive entity, which is reinforced by the fact that it is a projection of a single mind and personality in a particular time and place in human history. We can not solely consider the hierarchy of expressive "themes" in a work simply in terms of major "themes" and minor "themes"; rather it is the hierarchy of expressions or meanings in a work that can have very subtle, but significant differences which can create a highly complex situation. As we have seen, a work of art is dynamic, composed of different structural and expressive "layers" which are not necessarily parallel to each other and can be made up of a complex network between one layer and another with different degrees of counterpointing.

The Nature of the Creative Process

We shall interpret and trace the creative thinking which is evident in the works produced by Leonardo da Vinci, Pablo Picasso, Henri Matisse and Rembrandt. This will enable us to gain a significant insight into the principles and factors of art, which has been previously described in this course, as part of the dynamic creative process, giving them a fuller and more vital meaning. The analysis of the works will focus on certain critical features which demonstrate important principles of creativity.

The Exploratory Character of the Creative Process

In the sheet of "Sketches For The Madonna" (ca. 1482-83) by Leonardo Da Vinci (*Figure 122*), we observe that the master rendered several versions of the subject. This sheet of sketches has been considered as studies made for one of two possible paintings "The Virgin Of The Rocks" (ca. 1482-83) in the Louvre, or "The Adoration Of The Kings" (1481-82) in the Uffizi. In both paintings the body of St. Mary is in a frontal position. We notice in the sheet that the more completely rendered studies of the figures are the two with St. Mary's body that are in a frontal position (that is, the study in the center of the sheet and the one in the lower left hand corner). It is significant that one of these studies is placed in the center of the sheet, which strongly implies that it was the first one to be drawn for if any of the other three studies were done first the expression of imbalance would be created, which would be contrary to the basic human tendency toward balance.

The other two studies of the Madonna on the right and left of center can be considered as secondary explorations of two other possibilities that occurred in the mind of the master at that time. This kind of exploration clarifies the concept of the main trend in the development of a form or structure of a work of art.

We have reproduced Pablo Picasso's four major preparatory studies for the whole composition of "Guernica" (*Figures 123-126*) that lead to the final version (*Figure l27*). Except for the first three sheets in the series and the four shown here, the rest of the many studies are detailed ones of the various forms in the work. We shall point out various features of the development of the form of the bull. We will notice a constant difference between the bull and the fallen soldier and the dying horse. The form of the bull throughout the various stages and the

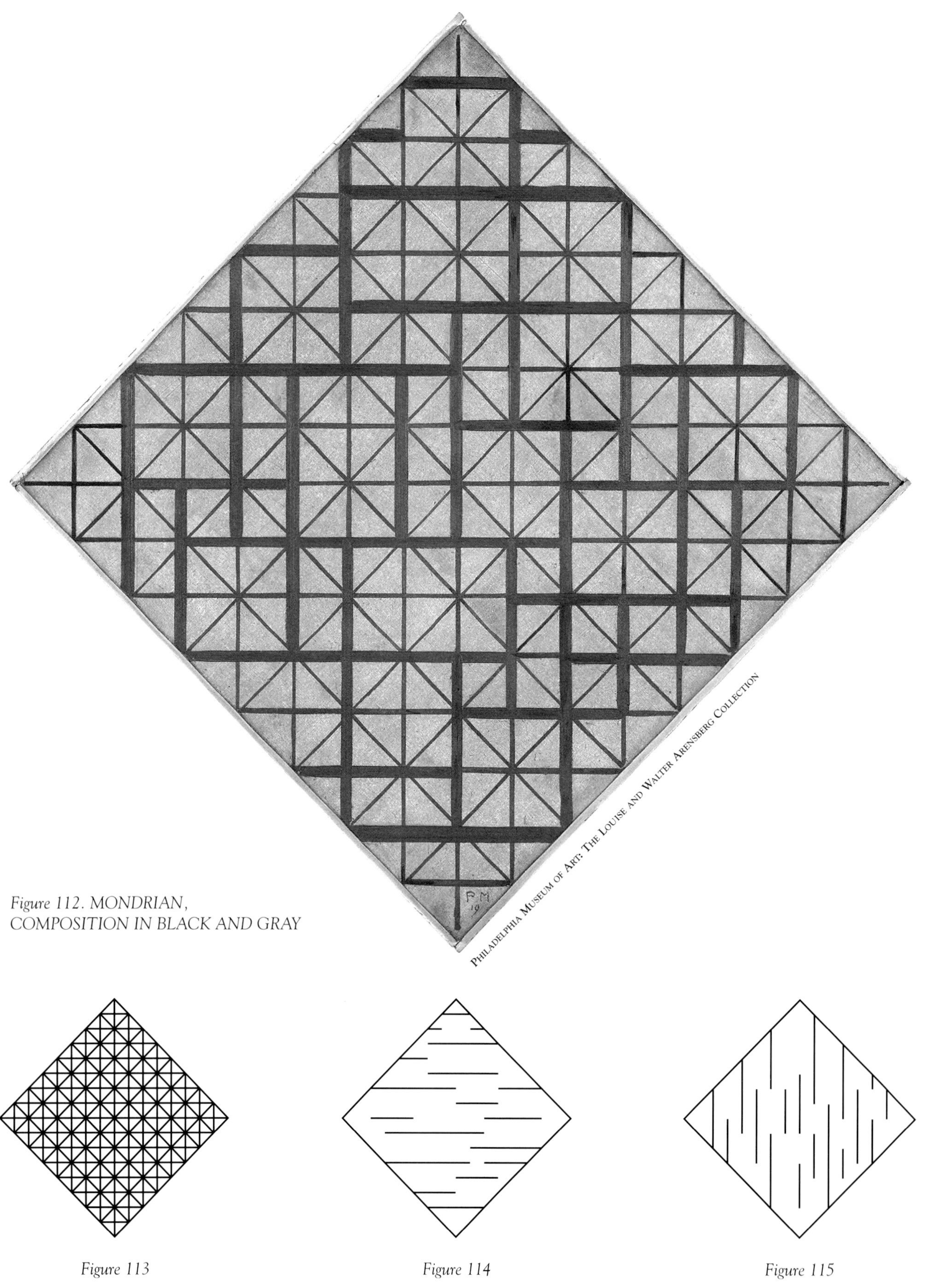

PHILADELPHIA MUSEUM OF ART: THE LOUISE AND WALTER ARENSBERG COLLECTION

Figure 112. MONDRIAN,
COMPOSITION IN BLACK AND GRAY

Figure 113

Figure 114

Figure 115

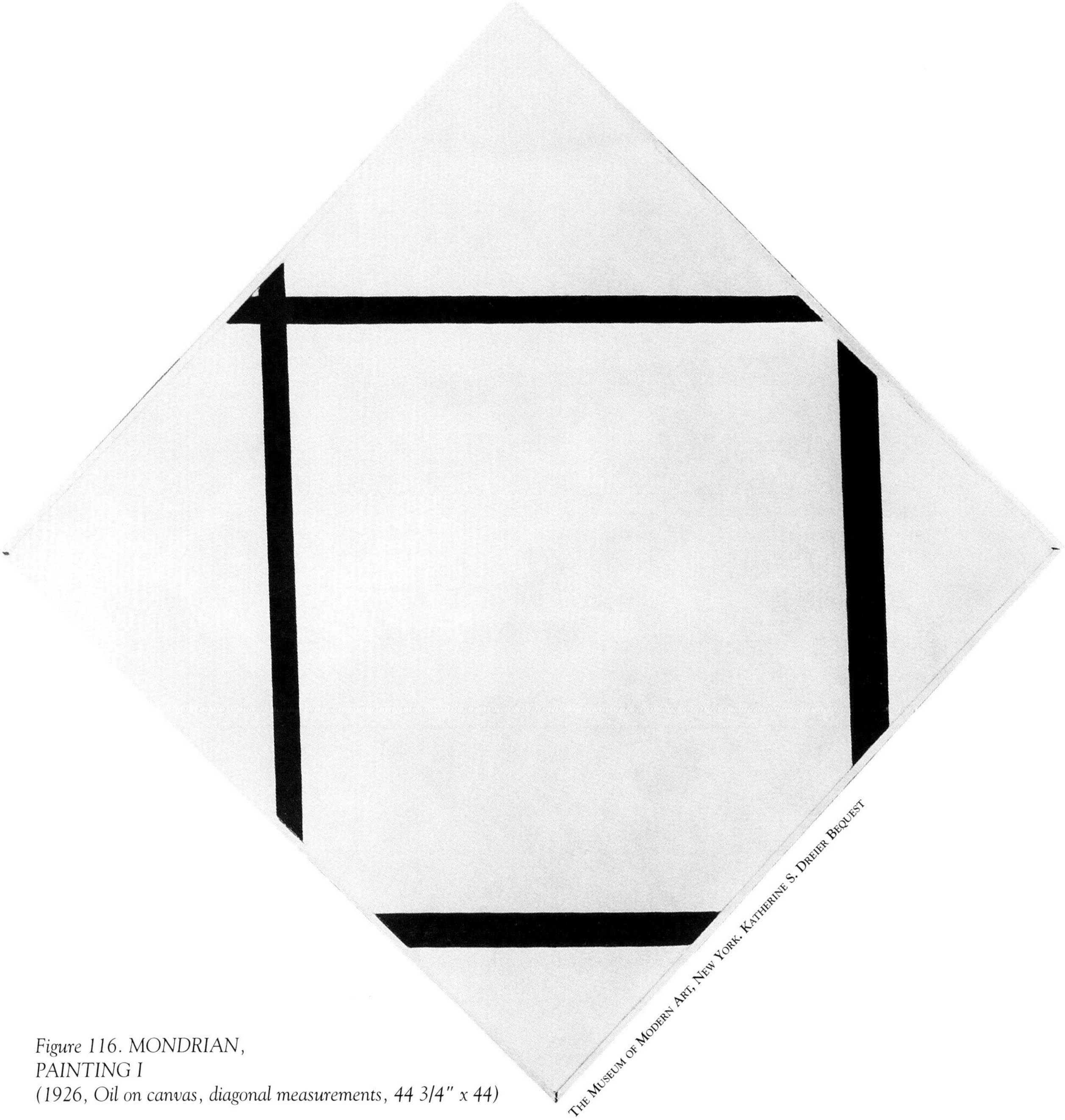

THE MUSEUM OF MODERN ART, NEW YORK. KATHERINE S. DREIER BEQUEST

Figure 116. MONDRIAN,
PAINTING I
(1926, Oil on canvas, diagonal measurements, 44 3/4" x 44)

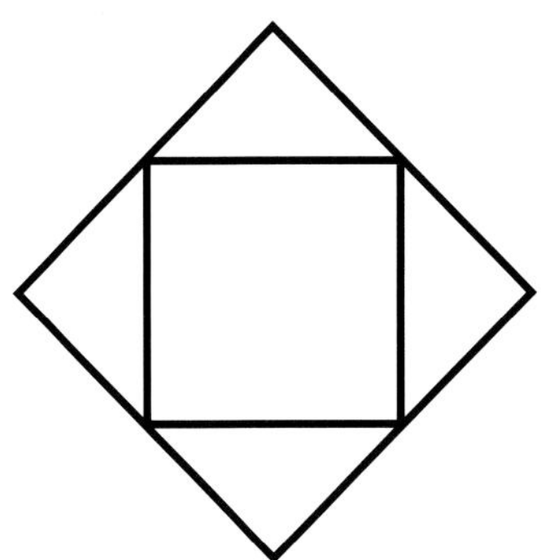

Figure 117

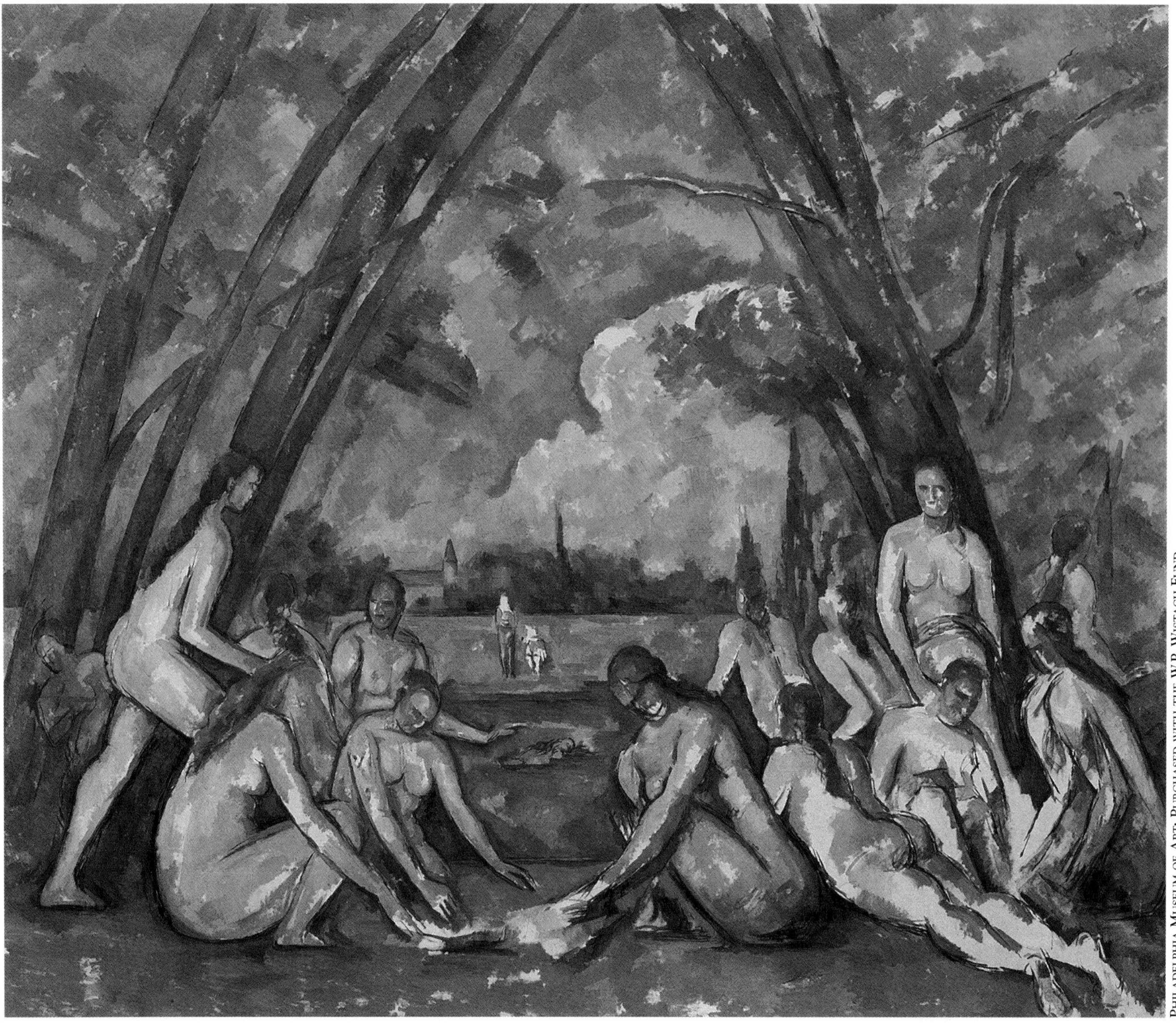

Figure 118. CEZANNE, THE LARGE BATHERS, 1906

final work itself produces an expression of "strength" as compared to the "tortured" or the expression of death of the horse and soldier. This is one of the constant threads in the development of the work which has the important function of being a unifying force in what may seem to be at first glance a creative process with very diverse directions. The general nature of the creative process, parallels that of a work of art having both unity and variety.

In the final version, we observe that the bull's head is visually segregated from its body, which has been swung around, through a strong brightness difference. Within this seemingly "static" expression, Picasso arranged the eyes and the sharp triangular shapes of the ears and the open mouth, giving the bull's head greater visual tensions and a more dynamic expression than was present in the earlier studies. Thus, Picasso incorporated opposing static and dynamic expressions in the head of the bull.

We shall first consider the simple factor of the physical position of the bull's head in relation to his body. In the four sketches (*Figures 123-126*), we notice that the general position of the bull's body remains constant, accompanied by changes in the position of the bull's head. In the view of the May 1 study (*Figure 123*) the bull's head is facing forward. The May 2 study (*Figure 124*) shows the head turned around. The

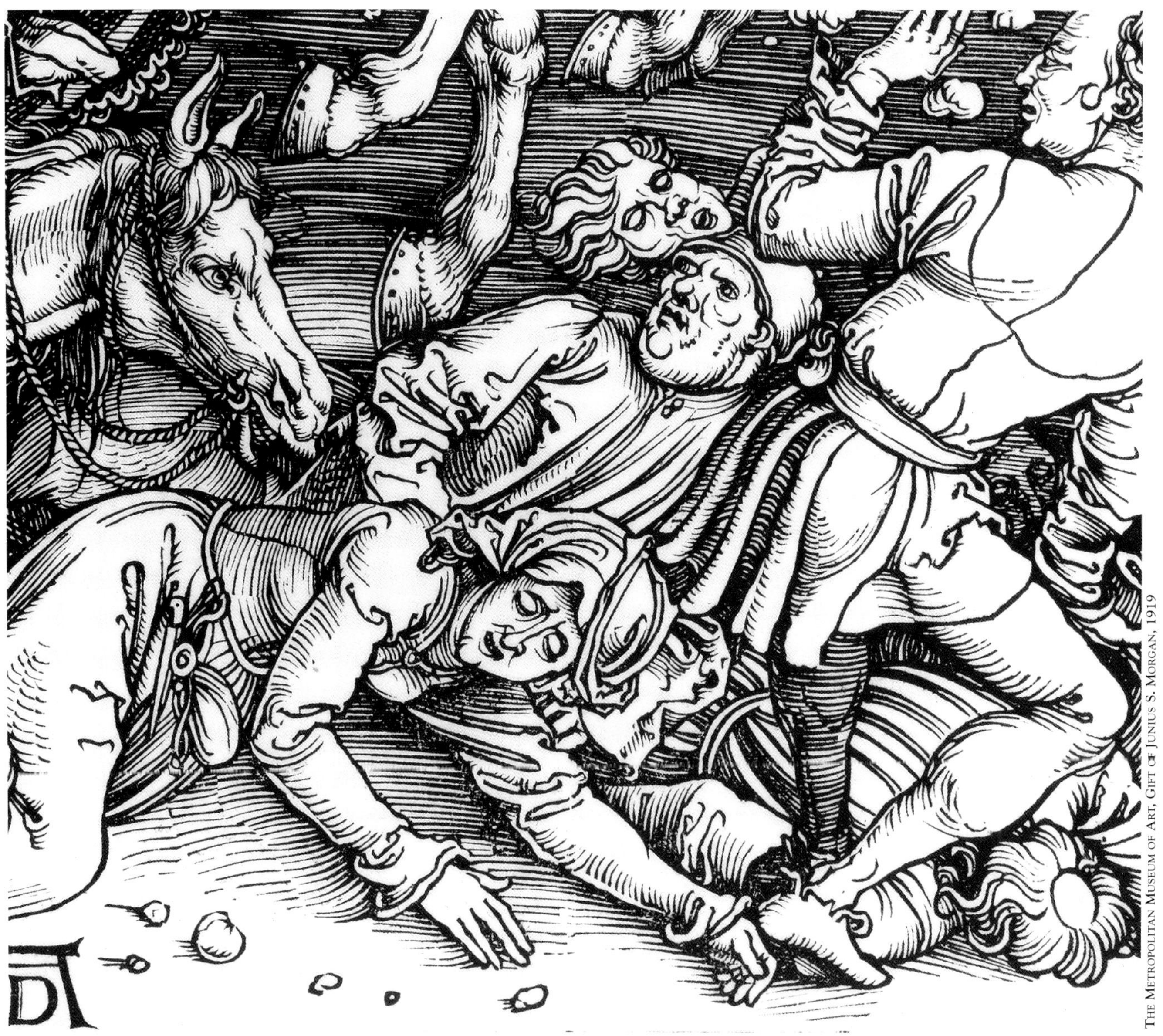

Figure 119. DURER, THE RIDERS ON THE FOUR HORSE FROM THE APOCALYPSE *(Detail)*

May 8 study shows the bull's head facing forward, and the study made on the following day, May 9 (*Figure 126*), shows the bull's head again facing sideward. In the final work we see the bull's head facing forward again. Here we see a rather methodical fluctuation and exploration of Picasso's two major possibilities of position of the bull's head in the work. We have seen the same kind of exploration of the da Vinci sheet of sketches (*Figure 122*). This approach can be called divergent thinking as compared to convergent thinking which goes to the final step of the creative process without modification of each step, while preserving an overall structural similarity.

We observe that in the studies of May 1 and May 8 the form of the bull has less visual tension. The bull seems to be standing in an almost "stiff", statue-like manner, his four legs firmly on the ground, with the whole torso and head facing directly forward, creating a general horizontal visual direction. In the studies of May 2 and May 9, the form of the bull is visually more complex and has greater visual tension and greater dynamic structural expression in comparison to the other two studies. We see in the May 2 study that the bull is galloping and that the visual direction within the form goes in various directions. In the May 9 study, we observe that the bull's body is twisted, one might say, into a very compressed U-shape, where we now have a

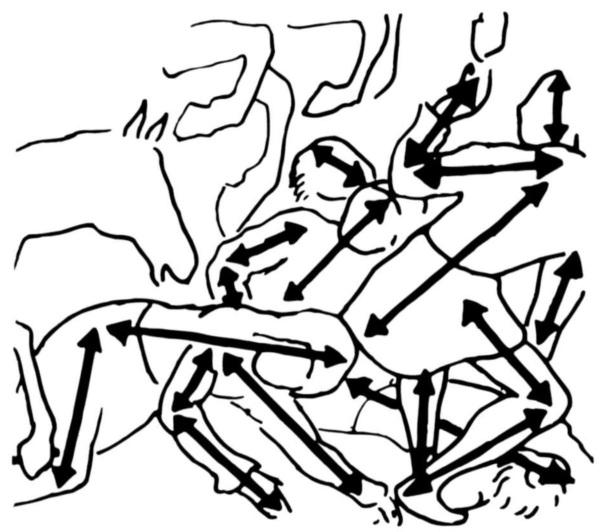

Figure 120. ANALYSIS OF THE DURER DETAIL OF FIGURE 119

stronger frontal view of the front and back of the animal creating a more dynamic expression.

We also notice that in the May 9 and May 2 study, the building in the background has a greater variety of counterpointing visual directions than the simpler form of the building in the May 1 and May 8 studies. We can see a unity of expression between the bull and, for example, the form of the building in each of these studies. In the final version, as we have already stated, the bull's head combines the two opposing expressions; we also notice that the form of the torso is less visually dominant than the head. The bull's body expression is therefore less dominant than that of the head. If the bull's body were equal in visual and expressive dominance to the head of the bull, a much greater visual tension would be produced, due to the sharply contrasting directions of the bull's body and head.

We have reproduced the four main stages (*Figures 128-131*) of the development of "The Swan" by Matisse. The etchings were done in 1931-32 as illustrations for a book of verse by Mallarme. We observe clearly a general direction which departs stage by stage from a realistic interpretation of the form. If we compare Figure 129 with the final version (*Figure 131*) we see how Matisse eliminated the muscle and feathers of the swan. Matisse began with a visually complex and realistic representation which he simplified step by step. This is an example of convergent thinking in creating a work of art. This approach is different from the one employed by Picasso in the development of the form of the bull. Picasso created a diverse range of structural and expressive forms of the bull which functioned as a kind of reserve on which he drew, adding some of the general structural and expressive characteristics of the earlier stage in each successive step.

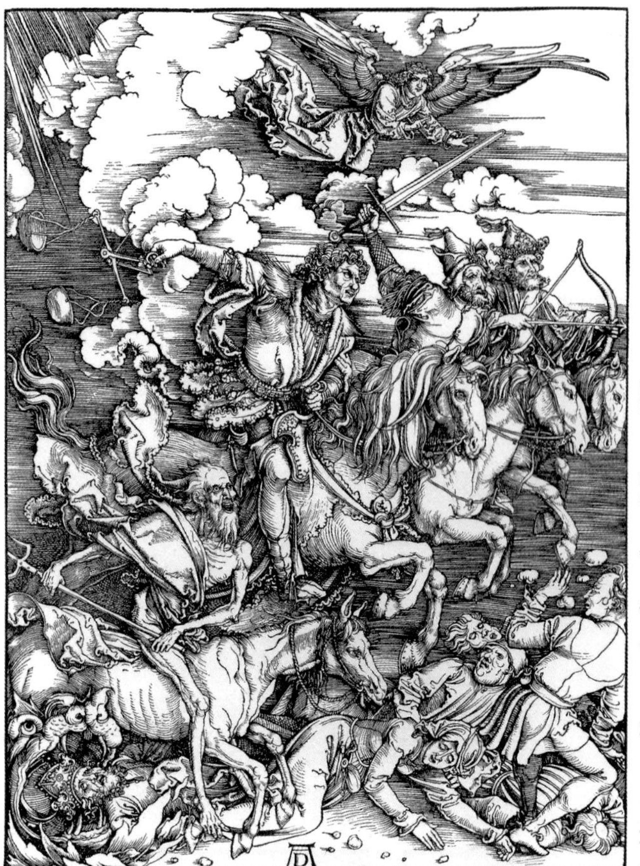

Figure 121. DURER, THE RIDERS ON THE FOUR HORSE FROM THE APOCALYPSE

The Concept of the Structural and Expressive "Gap"

The two basic goals of the artist: (A) to develop his particular artistic intention to the highest aesthetic value possible and, (B) to do so within the general character of the stable and pleasurable framework. The particular artistic intention, whether it shifts from stage to stage during the creative process or remains as a vague "image" which is steadily clarified, is of the utmost importance in order to give the development of an artistic idea a purposeful direction.

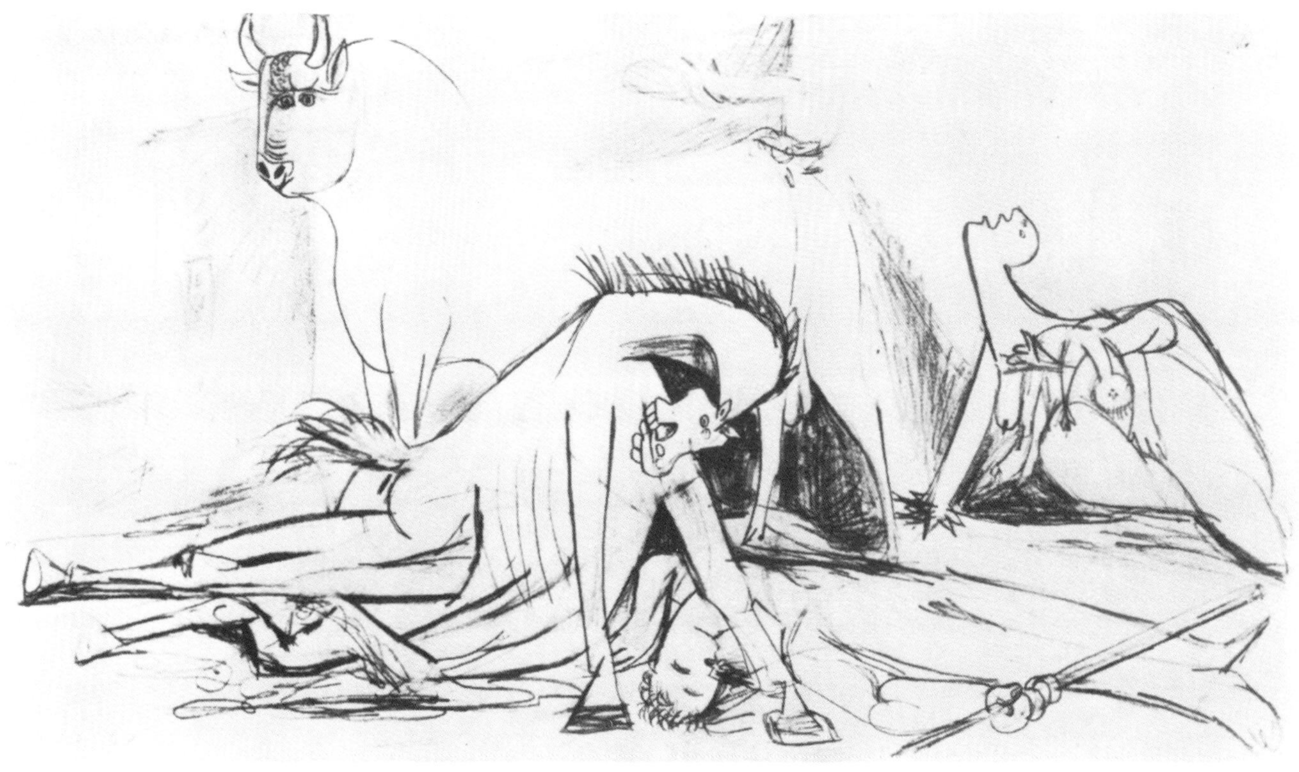

Figure 125. PICASSO, PREPARTORY STUDY FOR GUERNICA, DATED 8 MAY 1937

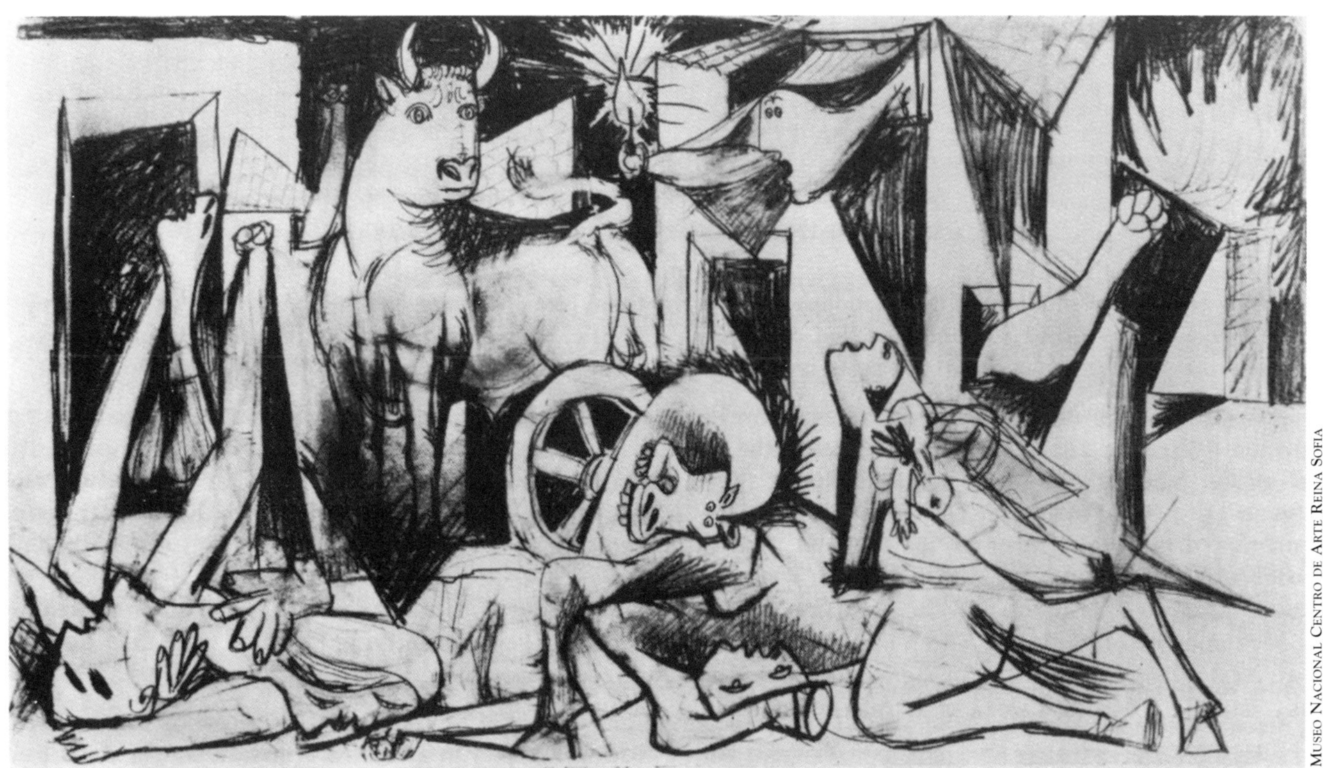

Figure 126. PICASSO, PREPARTORY STUDY FOR GUERNICA, DATED 9 MAY 1937

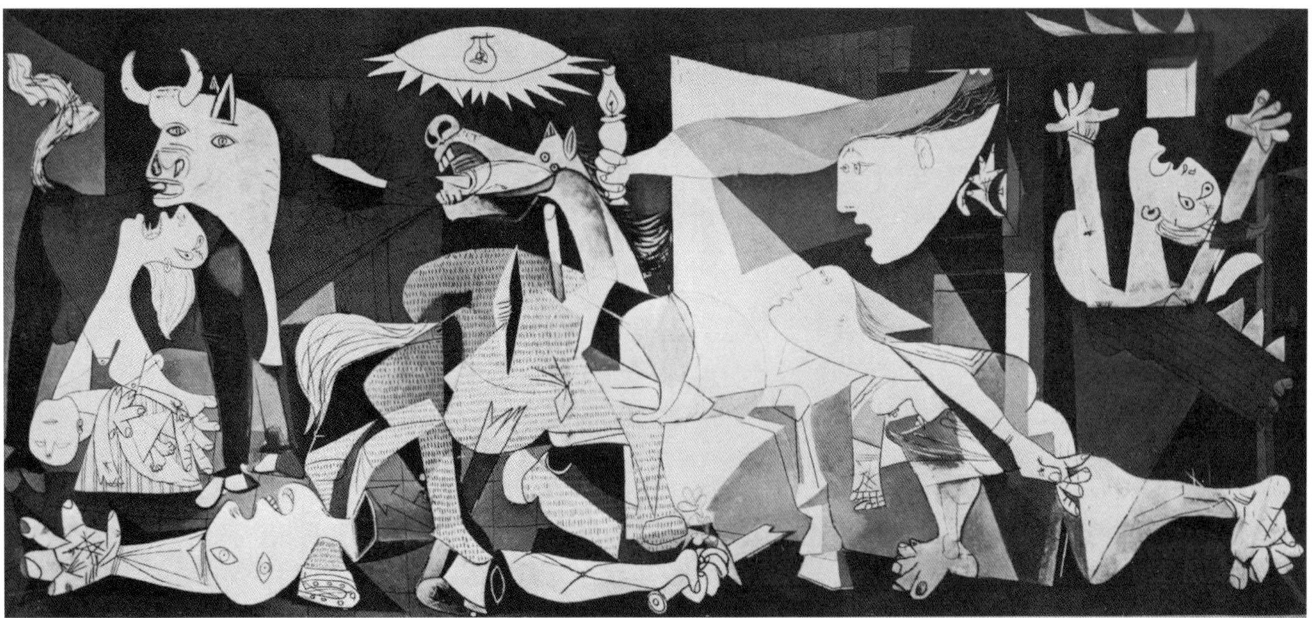
MUSEO NACIONAL CENTRO DE ARTE REINA SOFIA

Figure 127. PICASSO, GUERNICA, THE COMPLETED MURAL

We also observe in the detail from the fourth state (*Figure 143*) that the treatment of the form of the horsemen, next to, and to our left, of the figure of Christ, is visually flatter, especially the form of the horse, than the same basic realistic form in the third state from which it developed (*Figure 142*). The form of the horse in the third state occupies different levels of visual space, with the horse's head turning in space.

In the lower left hand corner of *Figure 142* we notice that the figure of the kneeling Centurion is a clearly rendered three dimensional visual form, while in the fourth state (*Figure 143*) we see Rembrandt entirely transformed its' visual character. Generally the form has a very transparent quality lacking realistic solidity. We observe especially that the area of the head is visually confused with the head of the horse. Both the horse and the man seem to share the same physical space which contradicts our past experience and knowledge of reality.

A study of the comparison of the treatment of the wicked thief in both states will reveal Rembrandt's bold translation of the visual and expressive character of the form, and cast light on the relationship of this important redefinition that took place in the fourth state to the generally established tradition of representing the wicked thief.

We will now clarify the basic symbolic distinction that exists in the traditional representation of the Crucifixion as reflected in the third state of "The Three Crosses." The good thief is symbolically on the right hand of the central figure of Christ and the bad thief is on the left. This symbolic distinction between associating the good with the right hand and the bad with the left hand is of ancient origin. The traditional depiction of the posture of the bad thief, prior to Rembrandt, is more contorted or tortured than the good thief which becomes meaningful through its reference to our knowledge and past experience concerning feelings associated with one's bodily posture. If we would attempt to physically duplicate the posture of the bad thief we would more clearly understand the derivation of the symbolic meaning.

We can see the parallel symbolic situation in the detail from Van Eycks' panel (*Figure 144*). We notice that the two thieves are blindfolded, thus making a symbolic distinction in terms of "vision" between them and Christ. The thieves represent limited human vision compared with the divine vision symbolized by Christ not wearing a blindfold. Rembrandt translated these kinds of symbolic means that have been used by Van Eyck into his own terms. We see that the bad thief is wearing the blindfold with his head facing upward toward the source of light which he cannot see. The good

A concept which aids our understanding of the general nature of the creative process is that of the structural and expressive gap. The gap is the "distance" between the present point of development of the work and the goal. The greater the gap the greater the tensions or stresses during the creative process. It is these tensions which can be called the motor that drives or motivates the creative process toward the direction of minimization of the tensions in the attainment of the artist's goal. What is experienced as a gap to one artist may not be to another. The gap is relative depending on the goal of the individual artist in his creation of a work. In this section two famous works by Rembrandt, done in his last period, will be cited to demonstrate the different levels of the concept of the structural and expressive gap that operate in the creation of a work of art.

(A) The Structural and Expressive Gap in Artistic Order: If we trace the progress of the development of the figure of Christ in the second (*Figure 132*), the fourth (*Figure 133*), and the eighth states (*Figure 134*), a detail from Rembrandt's print "Christ Being Presented to the People" which was completed in 1655; we will witness how the master closed the gap in terms of artistic order. (A state of a print can be defined as an impression or proof made from the same plate at various stages of the development of the work.)

The development of the form of Christ can be divided into two phases. (1) The second and fourth states which indicate the form in a very "sketchy" or incomplete manner, especially the form of the right arm, the cloak and the garment about the waist, which did not dictate or restrict the final artistic solution. Basically what is then established is the outline and location of the form in the work. We notice, for example, that in the fourth state the ambiguity of the garment about the waist as a visual form has been subdued. In the second state we know what it is, in terms of our knowledge of clothing. We can speculate that the tensions created in the mind of Rembrandt at this point in the creative process was stimulated by the structural and expressive gap, produced by the nature of the visual form. The form of the garment in the first state has a high degree of transparency created by the visually unrelated or uncertain arrangement of lines. The factor of closure does not function effectively here. Generally, the segregating forces have overpowered the cohesive forces in this and the other areas of the form. This situation lacks unity and tends to produce an expression of confusion. Disorder in a work invites the artistic need to order. Therefore the level of the structural and expressive gap at this point in this particular creative process is closer to the basic requirements of the stable and pleasurable framework, for the rendition of the garment is not yet a solid artistic form as in the final state.

(2) The final version of the figure of Christ (*Figure 134*) was motivated by the very specific needs of the whole work. It is of the utmost importance to note that the figure of Christ is the only one of the many figures in the print of the early states that was rendered in such an ambiguous manner. This was done for the specific purpose that Rembrandt reserved a more precise execution of the form of Christ till he felt that his goal was reached in terms of the visual and expressive character of the rest of the print, which changed dramatically by the final state. At this point, Rembrandt finished the form of Christ, unifying it with the particular artistic goal of the work which was finally crystallized. In other words, the level of the structural and expressive gap which motivated the direction of the creative process just before the final version was characterized by the need to fulfill the very specialized (or particularized) artistic order or goal of this work of art.

In the final state, the figural quality of the form of Christ has been increased through greater brightness difference between the darker areas around Him, and the widening of the dark area of the doorway. This development is significant in creating a visually solid and stable artistic form. The visual treatment within the boundaries of the form displays a sharp contrast with the earlier states.

Rembrandt has carefully integrated different brightnesses of dark, gray and light areas with shape and lines where previously it had not been. This form developed from a greater degree of segregating forces towards a more balanced propor-

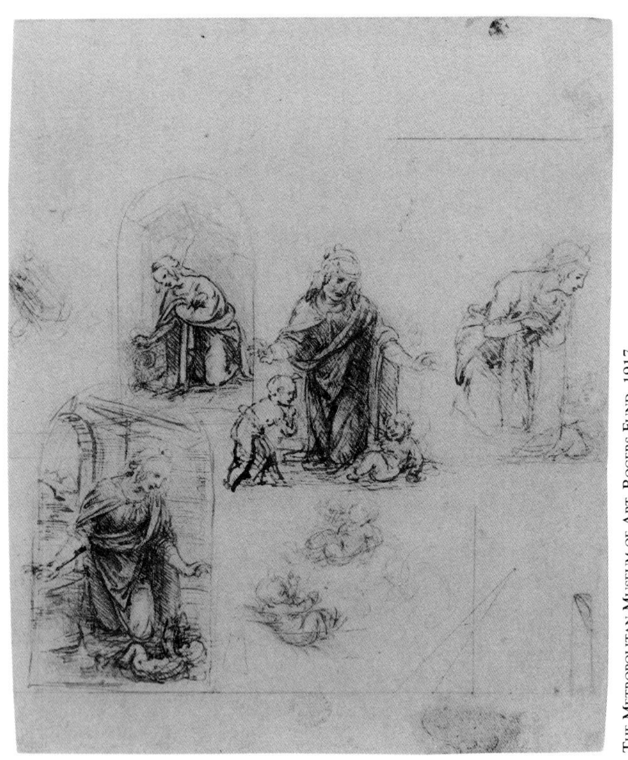

Figure 122. LEONARDO DA VINCI, SHEET OF SKETCHES FOR THE MADONNA

tion of unity within variety. The similar directions and shapes within the form are emphasized through the dark and gray areas in the final state contributing toward increasing the cohesive forces. For example, the direction of the left arm continues into the direction of the line of the robe over the right thigh, and this diagonal direction is repeated in the line of the cloak across the chest. This similar direction of the arm continuing into the robe is repeated with the right arm producing a criss-cross pattern contributing to the unification of the form. The shape of the rib cage is repeated in the fold of the cloak hanging from the right arm. The vertical axis of the whole form is repeated in different degrees within the form in the legs and the fold of the cloak hanging from the right shoulder. This arrangement or placement of the vertical axis of the cloak and the right leg produces a diagonal pattern or direction which emphasizes the direction of the right arm. We have seen how Rembrandt developed the form of Christ with a clear purposeful direction from a less structured situation to a more solid structured artistic form.

It is interesting to compare for oneself the head of Christ as it appears in the fourth state (*Figure 135*) to that of the eighth state (*Figure 136*).

(B) Structural and Expressive Gap Through Shifting of Artistic Intentions: Another kind of a structural and expressive gap is produced by the artist's shift of goals. An outstanding example is found in another work by Rembrandt, the third state done in 1653 (*Figure 137*), and fourth state done ca. 1660 (*Figure 138*) of "The Three Crosses."

We observe that both the third and fourth state of the print can be considered as complete and finished works of art. Approximately seven years later the master took out of storage the same plate and reworked it creating what can be thought of as a new work of art. Regardless of the great time interval between the third and fourth states the essential situation is not changed, that in both the third and fourth states the structural and expressive gap is at a minimum or non-existent in the work itself.

We shall now begin to describe the dramatic shift of Rembrandt's artistic goal from the third to the fourth state of "The Three Crosses." We shall derive our interpretation from the comparison of certain critical features between the states.

The most obvious difference is that in the fourth state Rembrandt removed a great number of figures from the work. This operation transferred the basic meaning (in terms of our past experience and knowledge of the subject matter represented) of the third state to a carefully chosen few. This reduction of the number of realistic elements (or parts) in the fourth state did not simplify the visual structure of the work. As we have already noted on page 21-22, it is the arrangement of parts that determine the character of the visual structure.

In state three, the general symmetrical distribution of the dominant brightness pattern is a visually or structurally simpler situation than the asymmetrical brightness pattern of the fourth state. In addition the whole character of the dominant characteristics of the visual structure of the fourth state has a greater visual counterpoint with the structural map. All of which created a greater structural complexity and visual tensions, producing a more dynamic expression than the third state.

thief is looking downward at the gathering of people around the crosses with his head in shadow. The light from above does not strike his face, in contrast with Christ's head facing upward toward the source of light. Behind the figure of the bad thief is a large dark area and another dark area directly below it in the corner. This large dark area implies a parallel to the symbol of the great blindness to the light such as is implied by the blindfold and the more tortured posture of the bad thief. In the fourth state these two dark areas are connected and greatly extended which has almost completely engulfed the bad thief. Rembrandt conveyed the same basic meaning of blindness (represented in the third state by traditional symbolic means) in the fourth state through the expression derived from the contrast of the dark pattern against the lighter one in which the figure of Christ appears.

Various forms in the fourth state have been redefined, and can be classified in terms of their different "distances" from reality. (1) The figure of Christ is most realistic. (2) The visually flattened horsemen in *Figure 143* is less realistic. (3) The figure of the Centurion is more unrealistic. (4) Finally, Rembrandt's translation of the traditional symbolic treatment of the wicked thief into a contrast of light and dark pattern. This range of "distances" from reality is not present in the third state. This variety of "distances" from reality contributes to the expressive complexity of the fourth state of "The Three Crosses."

To study the creative process from the point of view of tracing the degree of structural and expressive complexity of the different stages is another significant factor or tool in measuring the particular direction of the development of a work of art. If we compare the various stages of the works reproduced on the previous pages, this will prove to be interesting. (We shall use the terms simple and complex for the sake of convenience without any absolute meaning, only as a relative term within the particular creative process).

Picasso's first major study reproduced for "Guernica" (*Figure 123*) is simple, the next study is complex (*Figure 124*). Then it became simple again (*Figure 125*), then it was changed to be complex again (*Figure 126*) and finally it became substantially less complex (*Figure 127*). This kind of creative exploration of fluctuating between simpler and then more complex structure and expression is evident in other studies of Picasso. In the Matisse (*Figures 129-131*), the work became progressively simpler. Rembrandt changed "The Three Crosses" from simple (*Figure 137*) to complex (*Figure 138*).

The above brief presentation demonstrates two important points: (1) the application of a complexity scale, where at one pole we have a simple structural and expressive situation and at the other end a complex one, can add to our awareness of the nature of a particular creative process. (2) that there does not exist a rigid universal scheme of the development of a work of art in terms of a complexity scale.

Creative Abilities in Art

We have observed in the section on development of works of art some of the factors which are involved in the creative process. In this section we shall define the basic concepts of creativity. We have also designed a series of exercises, of which the intention is to develop part of the creative potential in the individual student. The exercises may also be used as an approach to measure this special aspect of the individual's creativity.

J. P. Guilford found that creative persons have three basic abilities: fluidity, flexibility and originality. In this section we shall interpret these factors within the framework of art.

(A) Creative Fluidity

Creative fluidity is the ability to produce a great many different ideas, although many of these ideas never become realized in the form of sketches or paintings. The sheet of sketches by Leonardo da Vinci (*Figure 122*) shows the master exploring different artistic ideas on how to treat the same subject. The creative mind intuitively and consciously evaluates, rejects or approves ideas, and this operation is an indispensable part of the creative process. Creative fluidity can not be truly understood in terms of the total output of the artist. There are many important artists in history whose productiveness vary from one another drastically. (What is important in art is

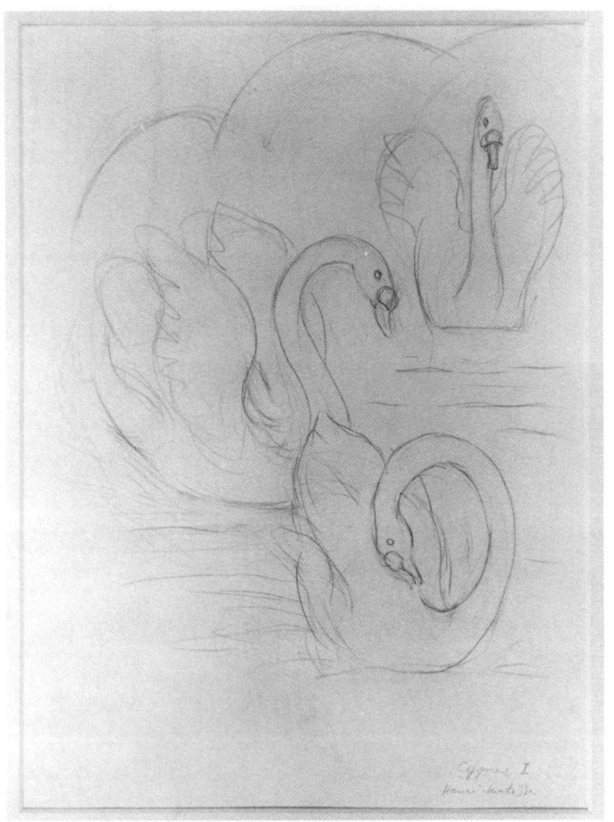

The Baltimore Museum of Art: The Cone Collection, formed by Dr. Claribel Cone and Miss Etta Cone of Baltimore, Maryland

Figure 128. HENRI MATISSE, *Preliminary Drawing* THE SWAN, MARKED CYGNES I

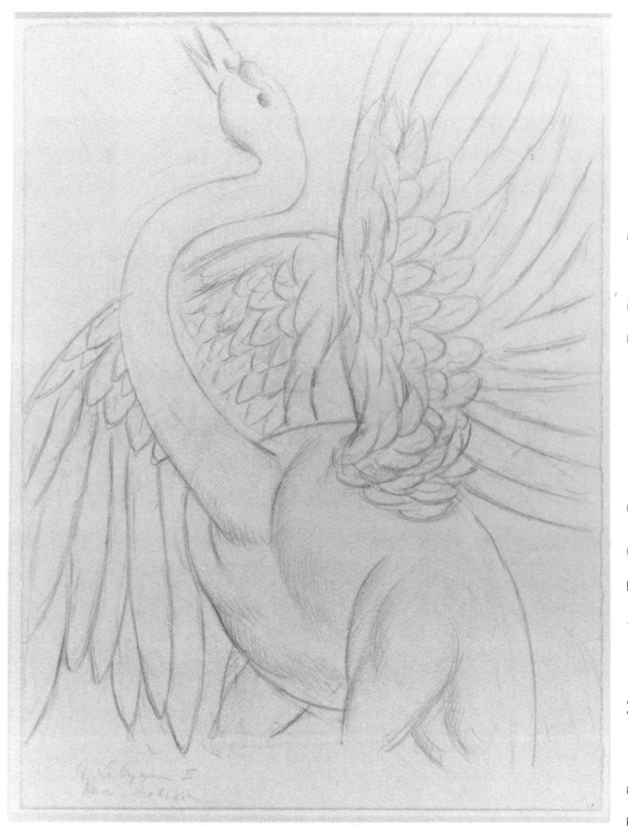

The Baltimore Museum of Art: The Cone Collection, formed by Dr. Claribel Cone and Miss Etta Cone of Baltimore, Maryland

Figure 129. HENRI MATISSE, *Preliminary Drawing* THE SWAN, MARKED LE CYGNE II

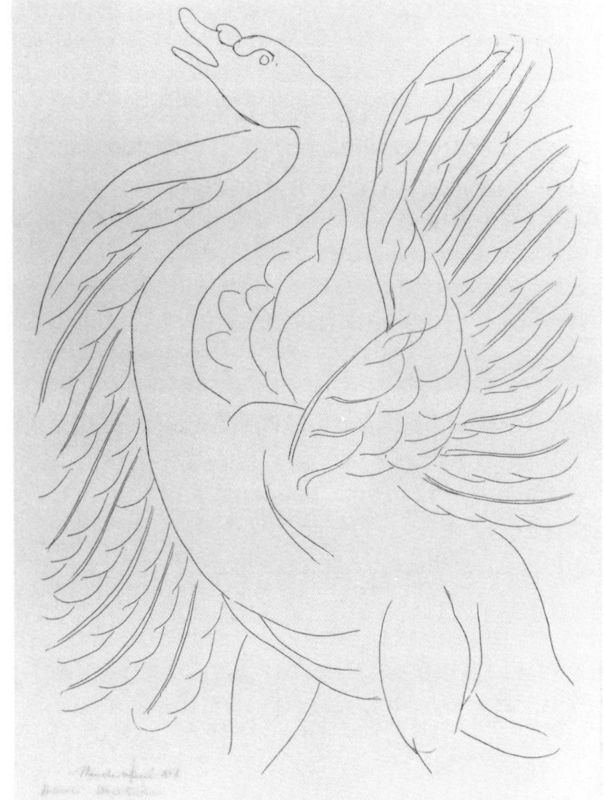

The Baltimore Museum of Art: The Cone Collection, formed by Dr. Claribel Cone and Miss Etta Cone of Baltimore, Maryland

Figure 130. HENRI MATISSE, REFUSED ETCHING FOR "THE SWAN"

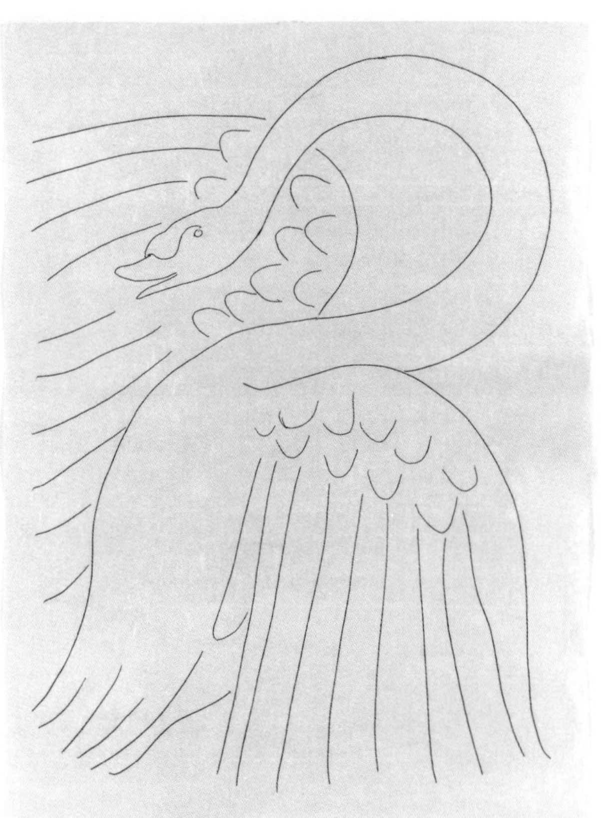

The Baltimore Museum of Art: The Cone Collection, formed by Dr. Claribel Cone and Miss Etta Cone of Baltimore, Maryland

Figure 131. HENRI MATISSE, ETCHING FOR "THE SWAN"

the esthetic value of the works produced.) Vermeer produced little as compared with Picasso. This holds equally true with writers and composers. The difference in actual production of works of art can be explained in terms of differences in the artists' personalities, individual styles and approaches. However, the importance of creative fluidity is to make available to the artist a wide variety of artistic ideas, from which he may then select consciously or intuitively. The individual's potentiality in this ability, as in other artistic abilities, can be stimulated through carefully designed exercises and projects. It has been found that, generally, the greater the number of ideas one has, the more likely a truly creative idea can emerge.

(B) Creative Flexibility of Expressive and Structural Means

(1) Creative Flexibility of Expressive Means: One of the main findings we have gained from our analysis of the development of Rembrandt's "The Three Crosses" is the concept of creative flexibility of expressive means. This flexibility gives the artist greater resourcefulness of expressive means, and therefore greater possibilities through which to realize his artistic intentions. There are two major dimensions of creative flexibility of expressive means: first, flexibility within each category or means of expression. Second, flexibility among the different categories. The range of flexibility among the different categories of expressive means can be said to be influenced by the historical period in which the artist lived. For example, the range of Picasso is wider than that of artists working at the time of Jan Van Eyck. This does not necessarily imply that Picasso has greater creative flexibility. An artist can demonstrate greater creative flexibility within one category than another using all three major categories listed below. This is true because, theoretically, within each category an infinite number of different kinds of works of art can be produced.

(A) The first category of creative flexibility of expressive means involves the manner of representation of realistic forms, or the arrangement of realistic forms. For example, expressions derived from the arrangement of visual forms may complement the meaning from or reference to our

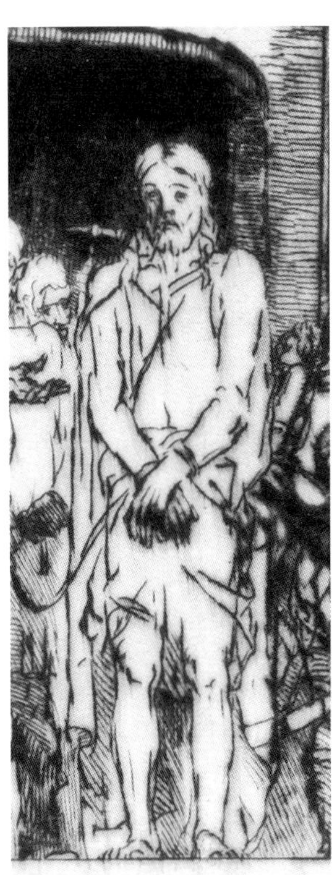

Figure 132. STATE II

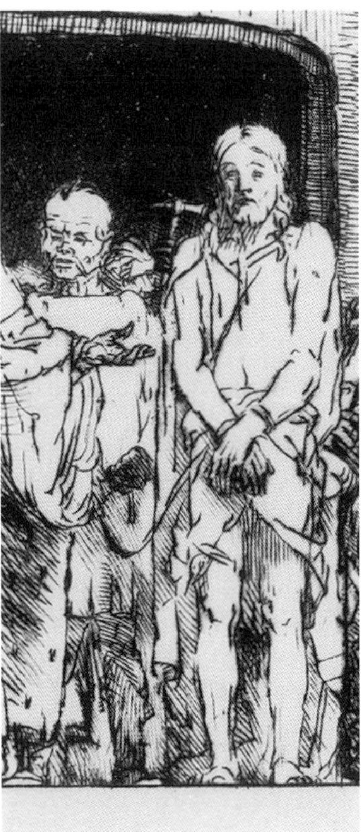

Figure 133. STATE IV

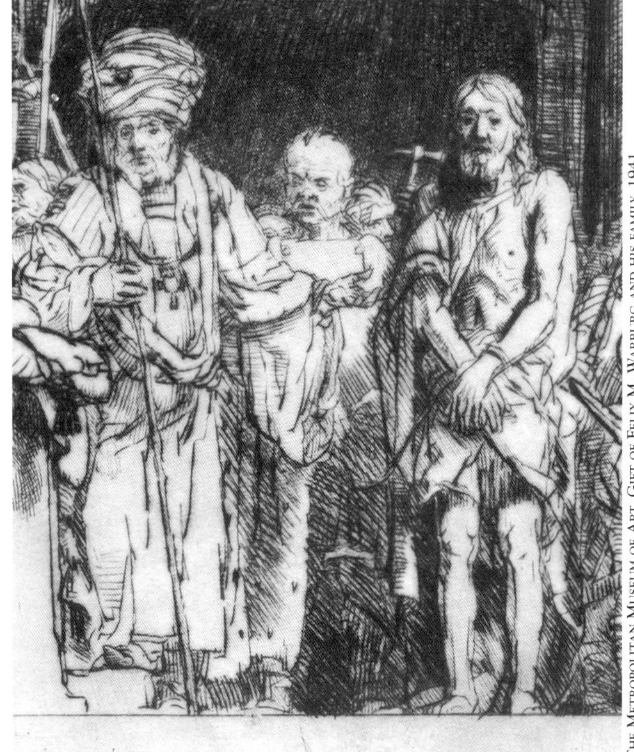

Figure 134. STATE VIII

THE METROPOLITAN MUSEUM OF ART, GIFT OF FELIX M. WARBURG AND HIS FAMILY, 1941

Figures 132-134, DETAILS CA. ACTUAL SIZE FROM REMBRANDT'S "CHRIST PRESENTED TO THE PEOPLE"

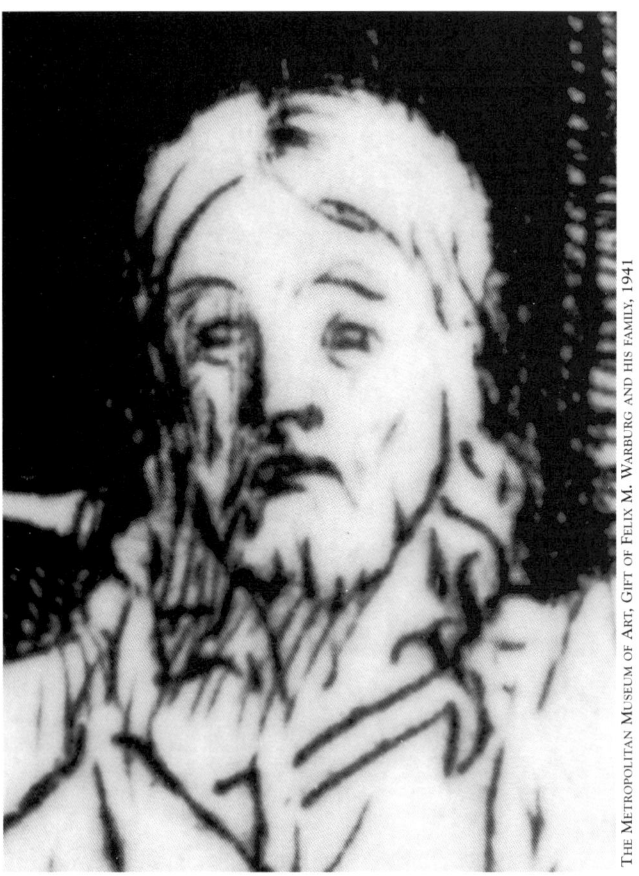

THE METROPOLITAN MUSEUM OF ART, GIFT OF FELIX M. WARBURG AND HIS FAMILY, 1941

Figure 135. DETAIL, CHRIST PRESENTED TO THE PEOPLE, STATE IV (HEAD OF CHRIST CA. 4 TIMES ENLARGED)

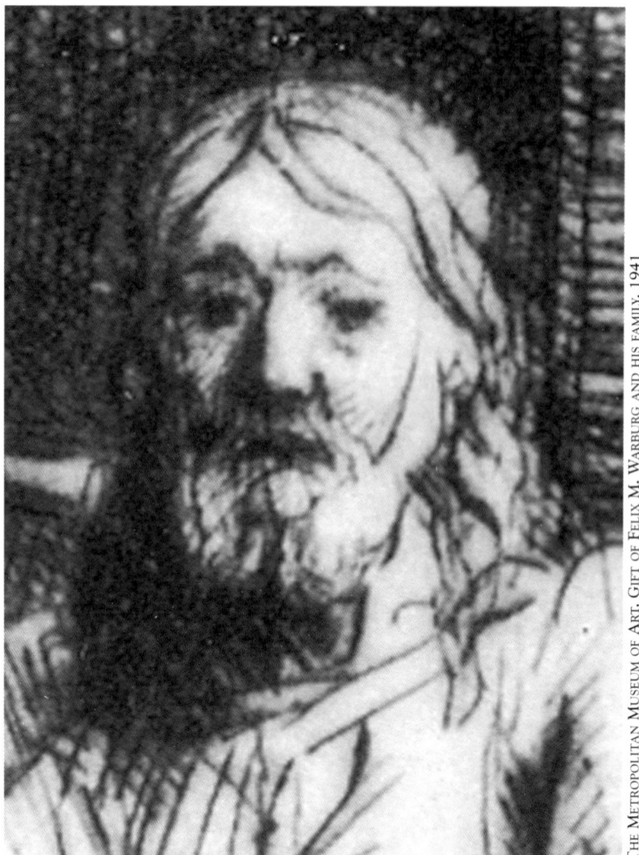

THE METROPOLITAN MUSEUM OF ART, GIFT OF FELIX M. WARBURG AND HIS FAMILY, 1941

Figure 136. DETAIL, CHRIST PRESENTED TO THE PEOPLE, STATE VIII (HEAD OF CHRIST CA. 4 TIMES ENLARGED)

past experience and knowledge as in the Van Eyck detail from "The Last Judgment" (*Figure 25*). Specifically the agitated expression derived from the treatment and arrangement of forms complements and emphasizes the meaning associated with the depiction of tormented souls. Our comparison of the Van Eyck with another detail of a similar subject (*Figure 23*) which we made earlier in the book, revealed that the expression of the latter is less agitated and does not complement the meaning of the work. When the two sources of expression or meaning in a work of art complement or reinforce each other, the work possesses greater expressive power. It is for this reason, that the masters throughout the history of art have preferred the treatment of expressive properties of a work in a manner demonstrated by the Van Eyck detail.

(B) The second category is exemplified by the fourth state of Rembrandt's "The Three Crosses" (*Figure 138*). The expression derived from the structure or arrangement of the visual forms, tends to be more dominant than some references to past experience and knowledge. What Rembrandt did can in essence be demonstrated by an analogy to the experiments of K. Gottschaldt on the "hidden figure phenomena."

The form of *Figure 145* has been hidden in *Figure 146* and it usually can not be found immediately. Gottschaldt wished to demonstrate that even if we know in terms of our past experience and knowledge that *Figure 145* is included in *Figure 146* we can not immediately find it because of the stronger visual forces of the whole, that is, the new arrangement of lines changed the visual function of the different sections of *Figure 145*. For instance, the three vertical lines in *Figure 145*, i.e., the two on the sides of the figure and the one down the center. Another example where the original expression of the part became subdued due to the character of the whole is the pieces of newspaper in Picasso's collage (*Figure 28*). (Refer to Hierarchy of Expression Section, pages 48-51).

As we can observe, Rembrandt fused the boundaries of most of the figures in the fourth state (*Figure 138*) within a new pattern of forms,

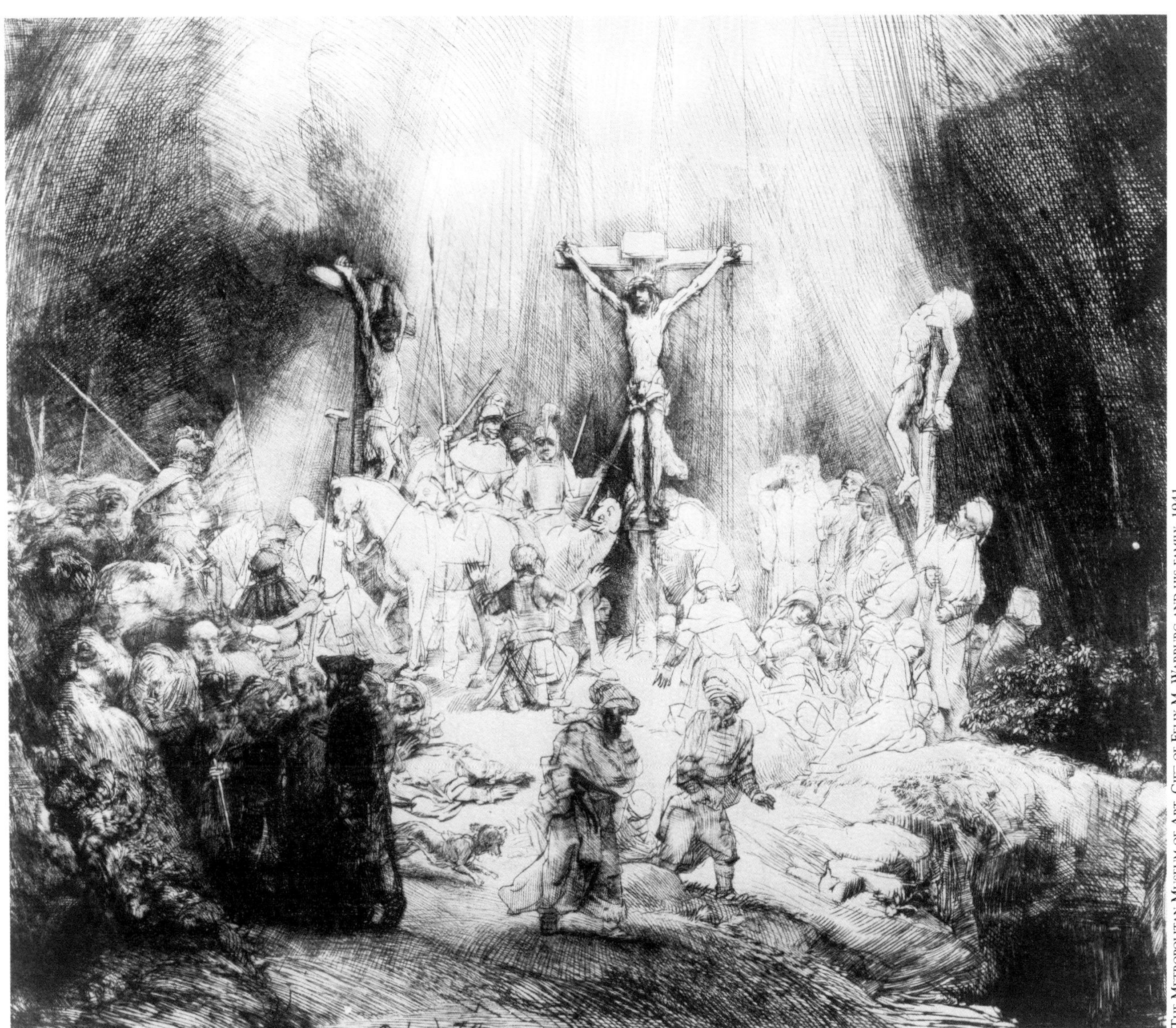

Figure 137. REMBRANDT, CHRIST CRUCIFIED BETWEEN THE TWO THIEVES - THE THREE CROSSES, (3rd STATE)

THE METROPOLITAN MUSEUM OF ART, GIFT OF FELIX M. WARBURG AND HIS FAMILY, 1941

just as *Figure 145* in principle has been hidden or redefined in *Figure 146*. This represents an important aspect of creative flexibility. It is the ability to develop hidden forms or patterns where the dominant expressive and visual condition of a particular stage in the creative process need not dictate the outcome. For example, Rembrandt produced an entirely different work in the fourth state of the "The Three Crosses" from that of the third state by further developing certain less dominant and subduing other visual and expressive features of the third state (*Figure 137*).

(2) Creative Flexibility of Structural Means: In the sections on the principles of Unity within Variety, Balance and Hierarchy, we have defined and cited examples of the major structural means available to the artist. Artists can and have restricted their range of structural and expressive means, treating them as a vehicle through which to carry out their artistic intentions.

There are artists who find they best express their artistic intentions through a variety of different structural or visual means. In contrast, there are other artists, such as Piet Mondrian, who after very careful consideration, has in most of his work deliberately restricted himself to the arrangements of horizontal and vertical lines, plus the employment of primary

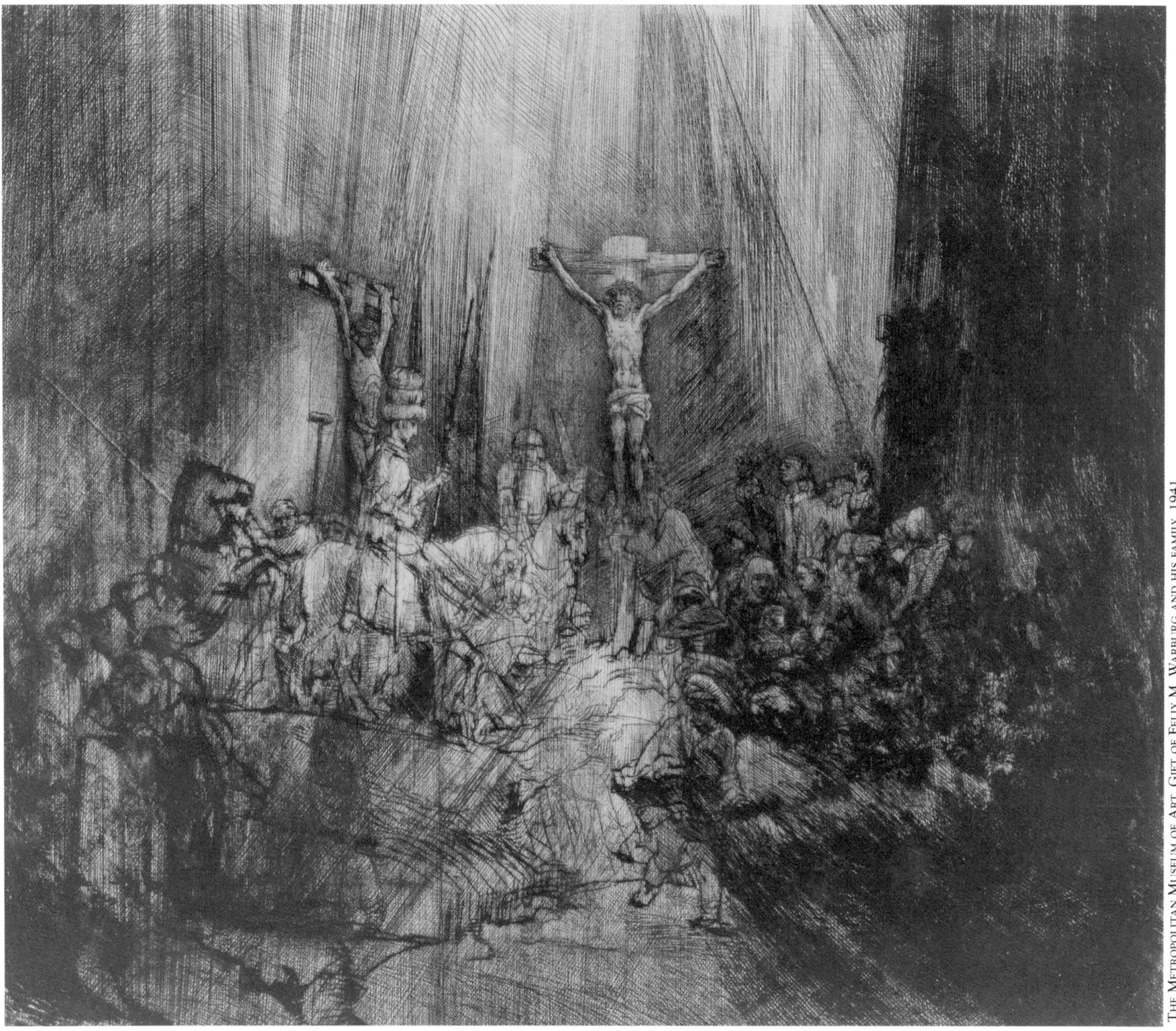

Figure 138. CHRIST CRUCIFIED BETWEEN THE TWO THIEVES - THE THREE CROSSES (4th STATE)

colors producing a wide range of artistic solutions. The mastery of the different means to express a similar artistic concept and the kind of ability demonstrated in the works (*Figures 145 and 146*) conform to the principle of art as an important part of the factor of creative flexibility of structural means.

(C) Creative Originality in Art

A general definition of originality in art is its remoteness from other known works in the history of art, or in a given group of works of art. Nevertheless, every work of art, no matter how original, may be traced in some respect to other works or traditions. However, originality must still conform to the basic principles of artistic order. A disorganized composition may be "new", but since it does not conform to these principles, it is not original art. (For example, if one says that two plus two equals five, this is new but it is not an acceptable solution within the framework of mathematics.) Creative originality falls into three major classifications.

(1) Creation of Original Structures: Originality of the structural appearance of the whole work may come about in two ways: through the rearrangement of familiar forms or by arrangement of newly created forms. Original structures may develop through a new movement or school of art such as Cubism or Baroque.

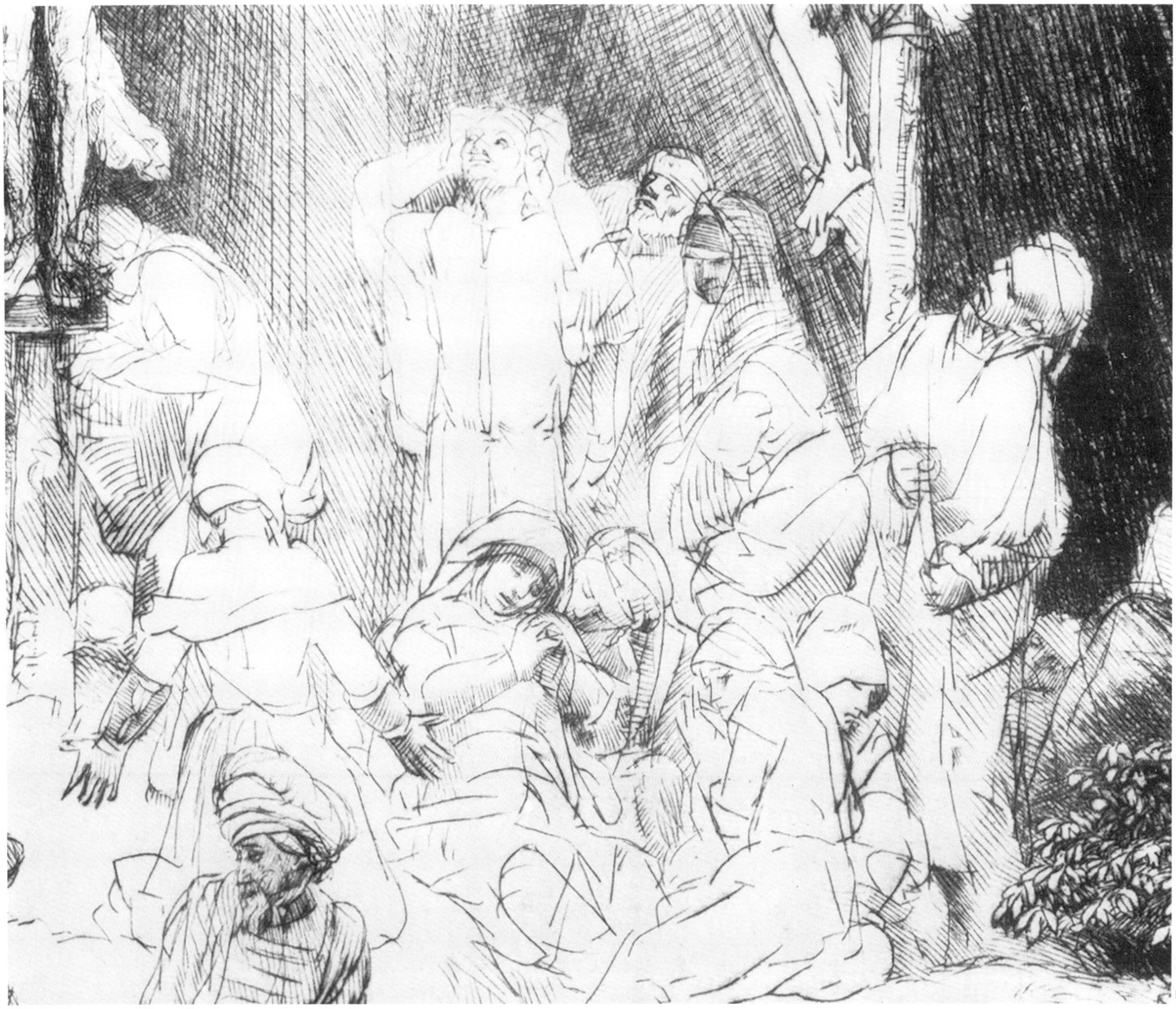

THE METROPOLITAN MUSEUM OF ART, GIFT OF FELIX M. WARBURG AND HIS FAMILY, 1941

Figure 140. REMBRANDT, DETAIL FROM THE THREE CROSSES (3rd STATE)

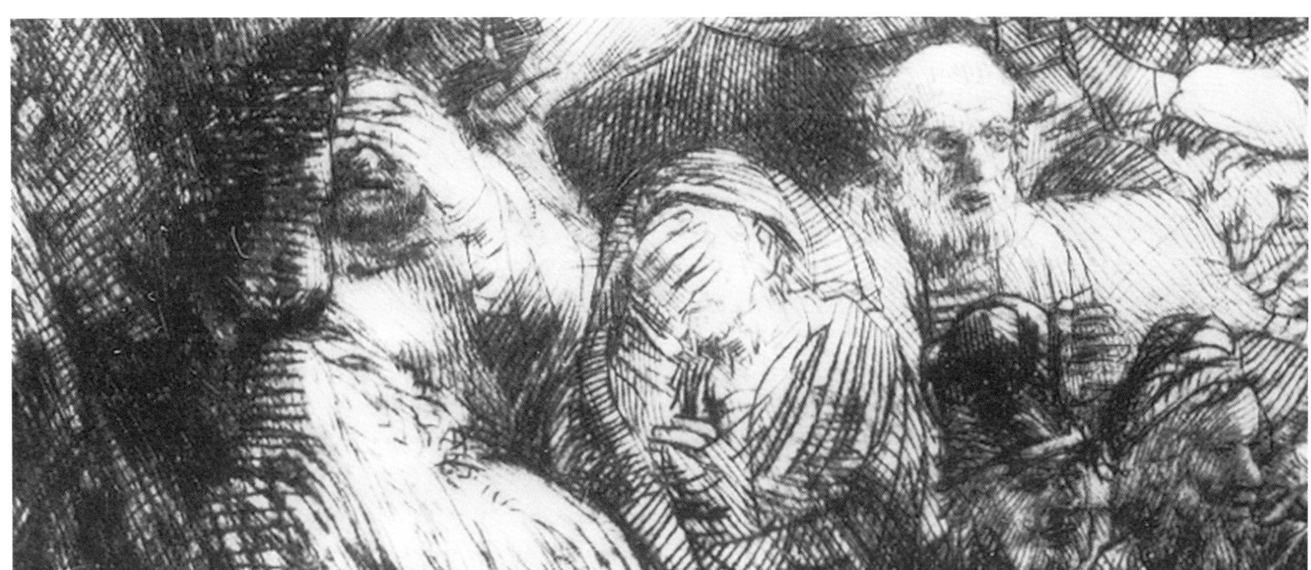

THE METROPOLITAN MUSEUM OF ART, GIFT OF FELIX M. WARBURG AND HIS FAMILY, 1941

Figure 139. REMBRANDT, DETAIL FROM THE THREE CROSSES (3rd STATE)

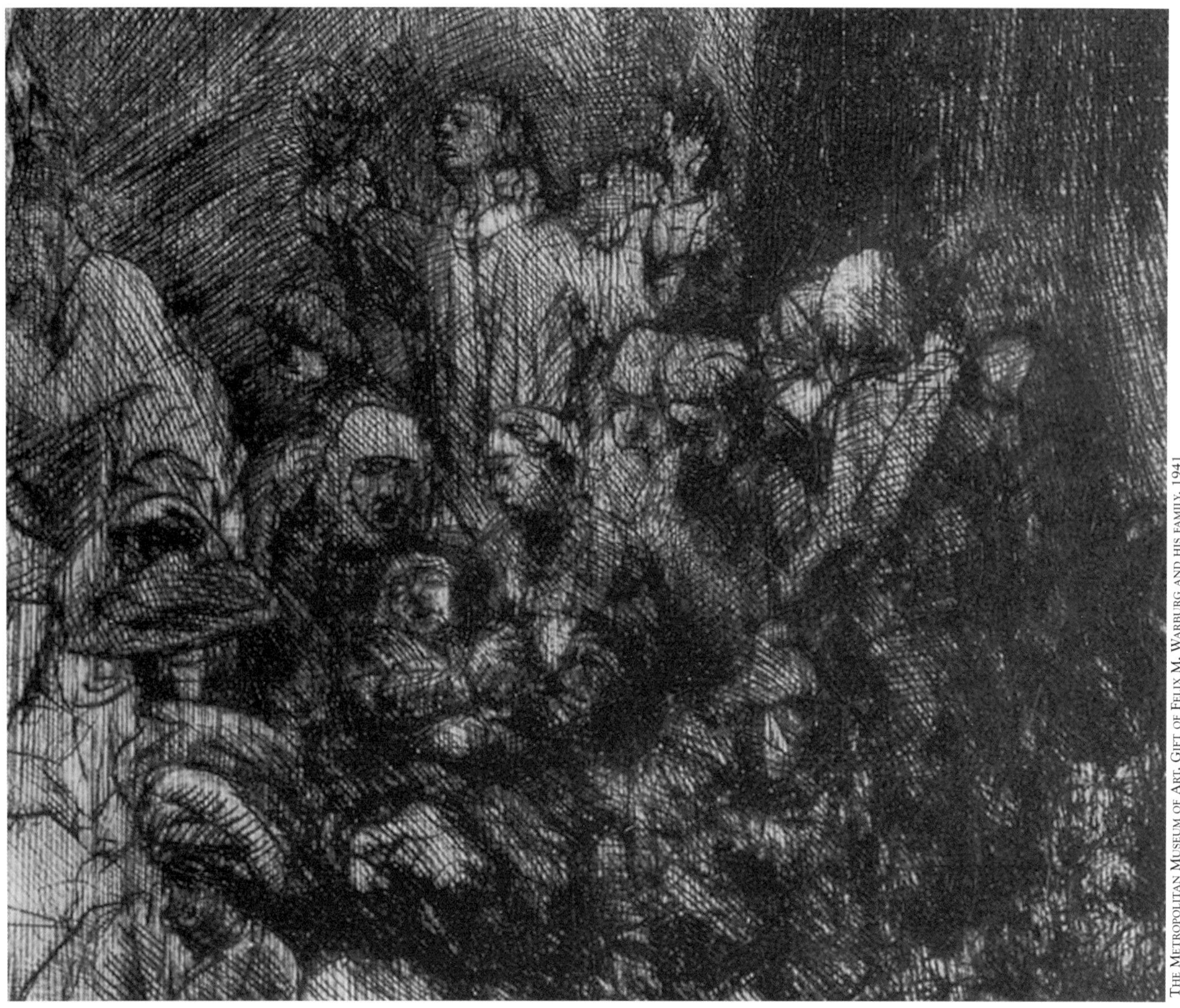

The Metropolitan Museum of Art, Gift of Felix M. Warburg and his family, 1941

Figure 141. CHRIST CRUCIFIED BETWEEN THE TWO THIEVES - THE THREE CROSSES (4th STATE) (Detail)

(2) Original Treatments of a Familiar Structure: Artistic originality can be achieved with a familiar structure which may have been used many times before. One may recall that upon first viewing of a good work of art, he has been reminded of similar structures or forms in other works. However, after more careful observation, he becomes more aware of the individuality of the work than of its similarity to other works. For example, one of the most often used structures in the history of art is the Crucifixion. Yet careful study of such similar works will enable one to see the differences in treatment of the form which gives each work a highly individual character. One may study the Van Eyck detail (*Figure 144*) for this purpose and compare it to Rembrandt's treatment of the Crucifixion (*Figures 142 and 143*). One can further study the subtler comparison between *Figure 142* and *143* of the "The Three Crosses". After realization of the uniqueness of each work, awareness of the overall structural similarity becomes secondary. We have observed the same situation among the Goya drawing and painting (*Figures 17* and *18*), da Vinci (*Figure 19*) and Picasso works (*Figure 20*).

(3) The Ability of Creating New Expressive and Structural Means: This category of originality is overlapped by creative flexibility. As we have already noted, the artist's range of creative flexibility of expressive and visual means can be influenced by the historical period in which the artist lived or lives. The degree to which the artist departs from the norm and invents new expressive and visual means is another measure of creative originality. Pablo Picasso and Georges Braque developed cubism

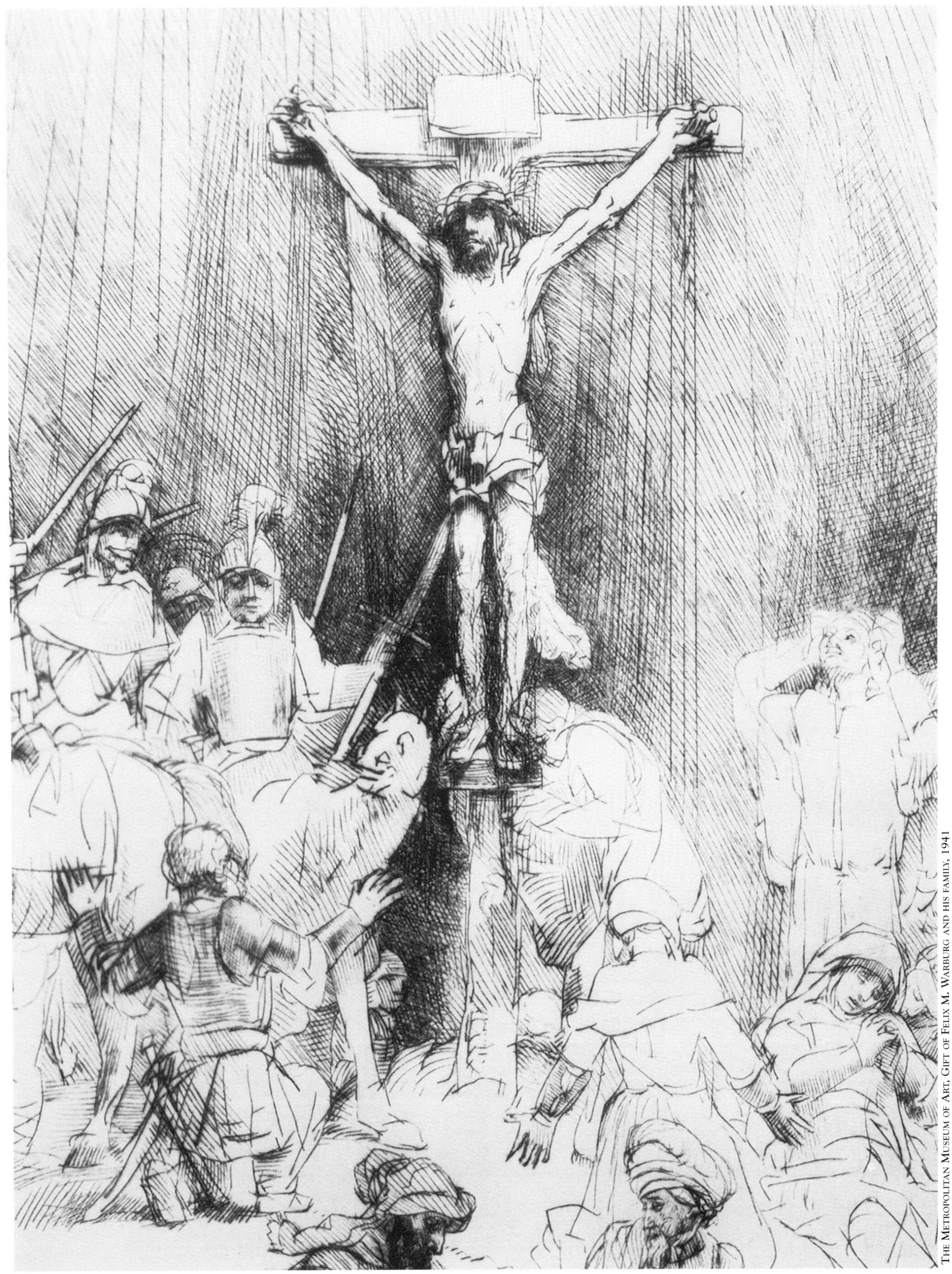

THE METROPOLITAN MUSEUM OF ART, GIFT OF FELIX M. WARBURG AND HIS FAMILY, 1941

Figure 142. REMBRANDT, DETAIL FROM THE THREE CROSSES (3rd STATE)

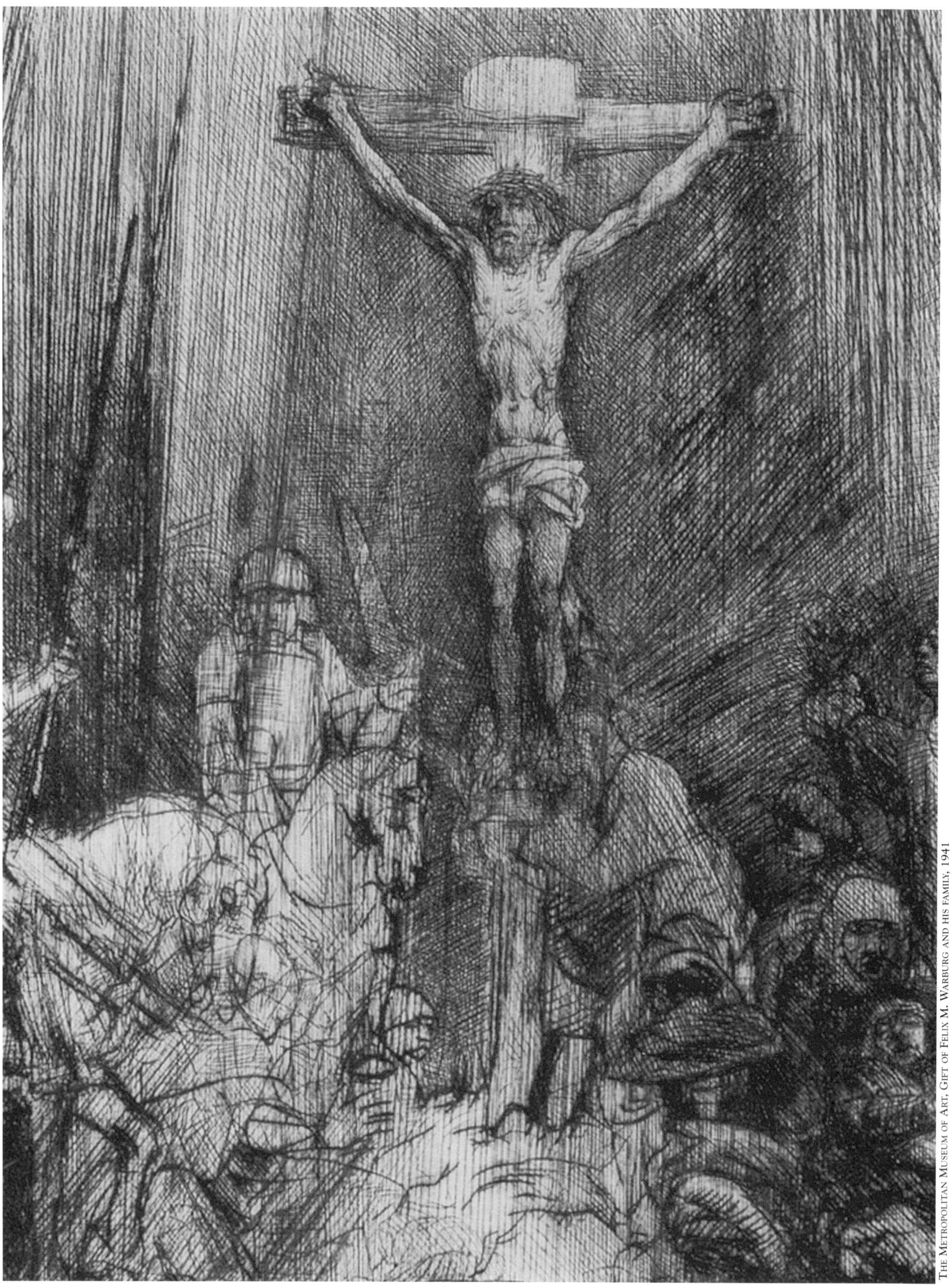

The Metropolitan Museum of Art, Gift of Felix M. Warburg and his family, 1941

Figure 143. CHRIST CRUCIFIED BETWEEN THE TWO THIEVES - THE THREE CROSSES (4th STATE) (Detail)

and collage in the early twentieth century; they are excellent examples of this kind of originality.

Experiments in developing Artistic Abilities

In this last section of the course we have developed and presented approaches and experiments which can be useful in stimulating the potential artistic abilities of the individual. These approaches were also designed to provide a means to measure each individual's progress. Artistic abilities involve the ability to produce creative ideas, to be able to organize them into a work of art, to analyze and make aesthetic judgments and to appreciate different works of art.

Thus far all the information and experience gained was arrived at by analyzing the principles and factors of art separately with their relation to the nature of the whole work of art. This section will call upon all this knowledge and experience simultaneously. This is necessary when dealing with problems and concepts which directly involve the nature of the whole work of art. This approach can lead to an enrichment of one's understanding, enjoyment and creation of works of art. It is for this reason that this section is considered to be important.

Exercises in Creativity

The exercises in developing the individual's potential artistic ability in producing works of art are based upon two fundamental approaches: (1) To have a stimulus or configuration which directly stimulates the artist in both experiencing and aiding the formation of a variety of visual and expressive forms or patterns. For artists have experienced similar situations when the work of art itself, or different aspects of it, function as a stimulant in producing creative ideas and to give direction to the creative process. (2) The other basic approach is a situation which stimulates the individual's potential ability to "think" in visual and expressive terms by unlocking or discovering artistic solutions. In other words, in the first situation the visual and expressive nature of the work which may have come about through the artists very careful planning, or by accident, creating some fortunate combination of forms that can directly aid in the production of artistic solutions. The second involves a greater participation of the individual's abilities coupled with the visual and expressive character of the work itself in producing artistic solutions.

(1) Exercises in Creative Fluidity

A useful device in developing the individual's potential in creative fluidity is to employ a carefully constructed ambiguous arrangement of visual forms; which does not have any dominant visual pattern and can be seen in a variety of ways. It is recommended that it be on a large sheet (i.e. 22" x 28"). It can be rendered, for example, with drippings of paint or with a mass of scribbles, made up of several colors. The task of each artist is to draw with the use of the same selection of crayons or colored pencils, as many different pleasing designs that can be traced to the visual and expressive characteristics of the ambiguous structure within a given time limit. The emphasis in the fluidity exercise is of the quantity of designs produced, not quality.

This exercise in creative fluidity can be divided into three separate kinds of tasks or approaches. (A) To emphasize certain visual characteristics and to subdue others in various degrees, without changing their arrangement as it appears in the ambiguous structure. (B) To rearrange certain or all the visual characteristics present in the ambiguous structure. (C) To approximate certain or all of the expressive qualities present in the ambiguous configuration, through arrangement of forms which may or may not be present in it.

This type of exercise can be carried out many times and may also reveal progress.

(2) Exercises in Creative Flexibility and Originality
(Pre-outlined Exercise 37-42 Sheets 8-10)

In the pre-outlined creative exercises 37-42, we have designed two visual structures which can be further developed into a variety of different kinds of structures.

It is suggested that each artist use the standard set of tempera colors: Red, blue, yellow, green, black and white in this exercise. The colors can be used pure or intermixed. The artist can eliminate as many lines as he wishes in the structure by combining different areas with a similar color. One can emphasize any, or all or none of the lines that make up the two structures. The basic task of this exercise in creative flexibility and originality is to make each of the four pleasing and visually balanced structures as different from each other as possible. Let not the dominant visual character of the structures necessarily dictate the patterns to be created. There are different patterns hidden in it which can be made more visually dominant. This factor was demonstrated in *Figures 145* and *146*.

To more clearly demonstrate the purpose and instructions given above, we have reproduced a sample exercise (*Figures 148-152*). We see that all the different patterns in *Figures 149-152* are embedded in *Figure 148*, and these were increased in visual dominance by simply combining the different areas with a similar color. The structure in the pre-outlined exercises 41 and 42 is the same as *Figure 113* which functioned as a linear foundation for Mondrian's "Composition in Black and Gray" (*Figure 112*). No attempt should be made to duplicate Mondrian's basic artistic means or solution, which he developed out of *Figure 113*.

Examine the work on two levels. (1) On the first level, note the degree of difference in terms of the visual appearance and means used in each set. (2) If looked at in comparison with other artists work, you may classify them in degrees of originality, from the most similar results to the most unusual artistic solution. This basic kind of exercise in creative flexibility and originality can be carried out again and again to measure and develop the individual's potential creative abilities.

Brainstorming Session in Analyzing Works of Art

The brainstorming approach properly used can develop the student's abilities in analyzing works of art. Brainstorming sessions have been used successfully in producing creative ideas and for solving problems through interchanges of ideas between individuals within the group. We are now applying the general brainstorming method in understanding the creative solution of an artist, i.e. the finished work of art. The important underlying principle of this method is that when an artist first begins to analyze especially complex works of art, there is the tendency to overlook or to place too much emphasis on some features of the work different from other observers that may result in a narrow interpretation of the work. Analysis performed in a brainstorming session will furnish a wider range of different views of the work, which can lead to a more objective and deeper insight into the nature of the work of art for each individual.

(1) Gathering of Ideas

The brainstorming session is divided into two parts. The purpose of the first part is to produce a large quantity of ideas on the nature of the chosen work, without any critical evaluations. Each person in the group should feel free to present any idea that comes to mind. For often times, it has been found that what may seem foolish may very well trigger a worthwhile idea in ones own thinking, or in another member of the group. It is important to try to combine one's ideas with those of the others to promote a direction and increase the momentum of the discussions. The work to be analyzed can be projected on a screen. An artist can indicate his analysis to the class, which can be accompanied by diagrammatical drawings. Another means is to use a reproduction of the work, in which case tracing paper can be used to aid in analysis. It may prove useful with whatever means are employed that little thumbnail sketches and very brief notes could be taken. The following basic points should be covered during these brainstorming sessions.

(1) Using all the information and experience gained in the course describe the dominant visual patterns and expressions of the whole work.

(2) The artist should choose one form at a time within the work, and explain his notion of how it functions within the immediate pattern and within the whole work. Describe how the visual nature and character of the forms and patterns contribute to the overall balance, unity within variety and hierarchy of the work.

(3) After all the basic forms are covered in the work explore the question: what would be the

nature of the visual structure of the work if a particular form was removed or replaced by a form of a radically different nature? Explore how this would affect the balance, unity within variety and hierarchy, or change the nature of the visual patterns. This will clarify the original form's function within the whole work. Quick sketches can be made showing the radical changes to demonstrate the effect of the work.

(4) The final portion of the brainstorming session should be devoted to defining the degree of importance that each pattern has within the whole work.

The main points are suggested in order to guide the discussion toward a fuller analysis of the work. It is however realized that there are times when an artist wishes to deviate from the outline because of a sudden insight into the analysis of the work.

2. Evaluation of the Ideas

Part two is solely devoted to an evaluation of all the points made in the first part of the brainstorming session. This session can follow the four main points suggested in the above section. The artist's critical judgments should be thoughtfully and carefully made. The purpose of an evaluation session is to delete, emphasize or de-emphasize ideas, that have been presented leading to a clear understanding of the work of art.

Brainstorming can be done on an individual level by first listing all the possibilities that come to one's mind,which then is followed by carefully applied critical judgments. Brainstorming can take the form of a written report and structural analysis of the work. One can use Rembrandt's "Descent from the Cross by Torchlight" (*Figure 153*) or reproductions of works of art which have not been fully analyzed in this book for the brainstorming session.

Exercises in Developing Aesthetic Judgement

One way to develop the individual's potential is to make critical judgments through increasing understanding and experience in studying works of art. Another important method is to submit or test one's judgment of a work of art under a carefully planned series of different conditions. That is, alter the framework within which the judgment is made.

The particular method outlined below was based upon the extensive research on adaptation level as a frame of reference in making judgments which was carried out by Harry Helson. We are not concerned with questions of the artist's "rightness" or "acceptability" or "conformity" to some opinion, but presents an approach through which the artist can be exposed to a carefully planned sequence of artistic experiences and in stimulating aesthetic judgments.

PHASE 1

The first exercise is to have each artist make a judgment of one work of art that he knows from his experience and that he regards very highly and another of one that he considers to be very poor. This choice must be made entirely by the artist himself without informing anyone of it. If the artist wishes, he may find examples in magazines. He may choose from reproductions of works of art, advertisements, etc. The works may be in black or white or in full color. On the back of each reproduction should be written the artist's name and his judgment of the work as "best" or "worst".

For each work chosen, the student should use tracing paper to make a careful structural analysis. After this analysis, the student will be more aware of the specific identity, or exact nature of the work. He may then alter his judgment. If this occurs, he should write out his reasons for the new judgment and search again for examples of the "best" and the "worst".

We shall suggest questions which the student can consider (there are additional points which may occur to the student.)

1. Does the work adhere to the fundamental principles of art?

2. What is your attitude toward the particular structural and expressive means the artist used to create the work?

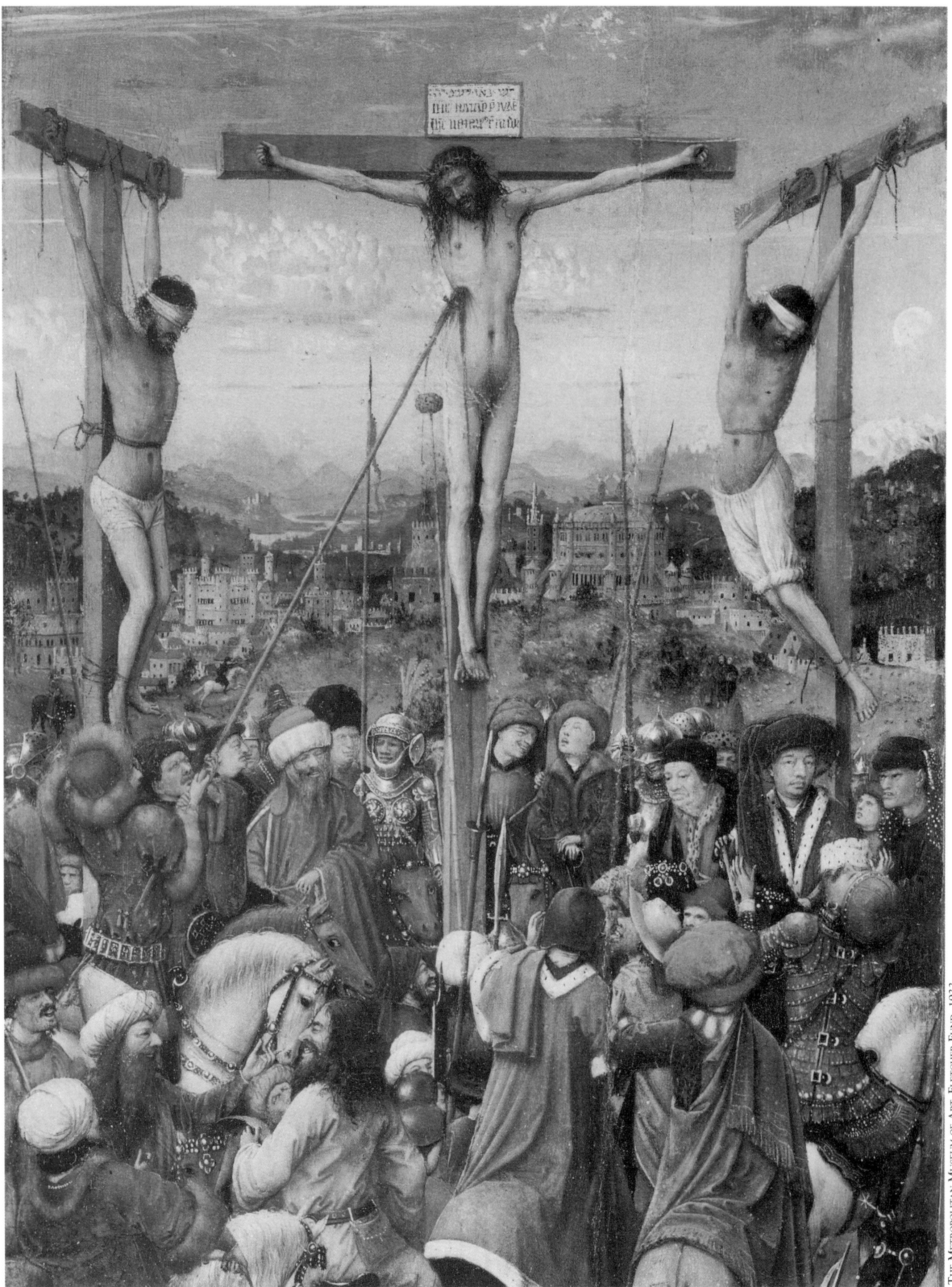

The Metropolitan Museum of Art, Fletcher Fund, 1933

Figure 144. JAN VAN EYCK, THE CRUCIFIXION (Detail)

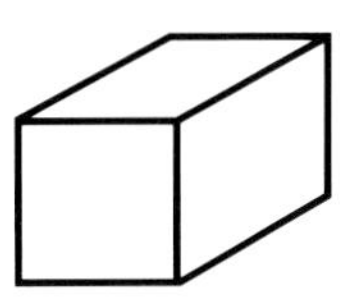

Figure145

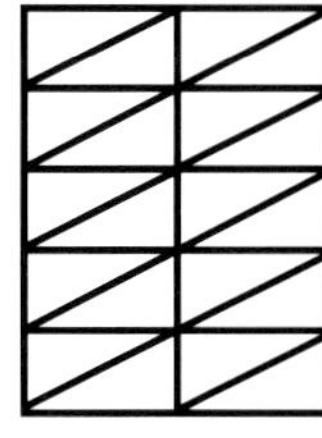

Figure 146

3. How much do you consider the work to be creative?

4. Is there anything which you consider especially awkward or unappealing or masterful in the work? (Indicate this in your structural analysis.) Also, one may show how the disturbing example could be improved and how the structure of the masterful example could be altered so that it would no longer be masterful. Make drawings of these, also.

5. Do you believe the artists' intentions were realized in his work?

6. What particular aspect of expression or meaning do you consider to be most impressive or lack power in each of your choices.

7. In the final step this can test one's grasp of the problem and also can prove to be a useful method to begin developing the ability to organize works of art.

(a) Indicate on the tracing paper placed over one's choice of the "worst example" how it can be improved by modifying existing features by deleting one and/or more features and/or adding new features.

(b) Indicate on tracing paper placed over one's choice of "best example" how it can be devalued by modifying existing features and/or deleting one or more features and/or adding new features.

These basic questions plus others that one personally regard as important should be used as a guide throughout the judgment exercises.

PHASE II

A. After the teacher collects and studies the choices and reasons, which will be valuable in stimulating the discussion period to follow, he should number every work that was handed in and hang them up on the class room wall with the structural analysis and notes along side. He should not disclose whose choices are represented.

B. The next step is to have the students study them, making notes and sketches, if necessary, without, however, conversing with other students. Afterwards, each student should consider objectively, if he found an example inferior to his choice of the "worst" or superior to their original choice of the "best". This allows the student to reconsider his original choice within a new framework, consisting of works which may not be known to him. Then the student is to record his earlier choice, by number or title of the example, and, if there are any changes in judgment, indicate the new choice on paper. He should give this, too, to his teacher.

C. A class discussion should follow these exercises with this procedure. Begin with one student at a time to present his reasons for his choice or change of choice, to be met with the opposing or concurring opinions of the rest of the class. This will tend to provide a larger range of consideration than that which the individual may have on his own. During the discussion period, in which the opinions of the others are being expressed, the student whose views are being discussed will not participate in the discussion. His attitude should be to carefully consider what each person has said and to objectively try to understand the root of their reasons. After all the opinions have been given, he may then present some of his reactions. By the time several pictures and opinions are presented and discussed in such a manner, a very wide base of considerations should have been presented, which can contribute to the enrichment of the individuals judgments.

D. After his discussion is completed, each student should make a note to indicate any change in his choice of works. The teacher may take a poll of the individual judgments at this point to note the degree of changes. In evaluating the poll, agreement or lack of agreement among the members of the class is not significant. Later, one should consider the

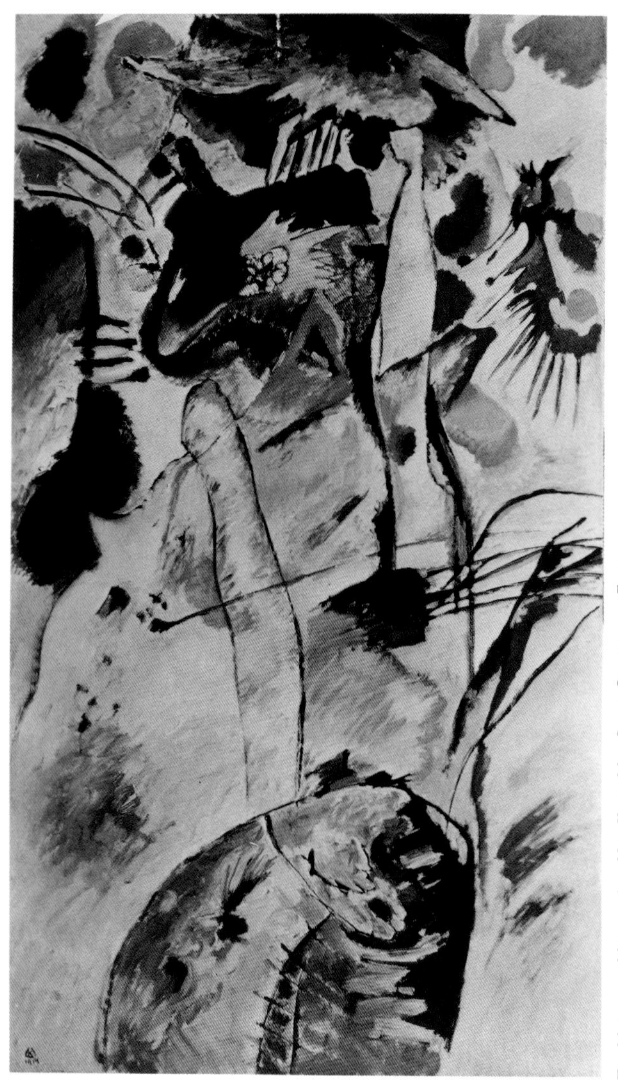

THE MUSEUM OF MODERN ART, NEW YORK. MRS. SIMON GUGGENHEIM FUND

Figure 147. VASILY KANDINSKY, PANEL FOR EDWIN R. CAMPBELL NO. 1 (1914, Oil on canvas, 64" x 36 1/4")

degree of changes and whether the changes have resulted from the introduction of new factors to the approach of the individual; or, if the judgments have remained unchanged, whether the judgments now rests on a richer set of reasons.

PHASE III Standard Set of Works to Be Judged:

It is suggested that the teacher, at this point, (a) choose a set of five to ten works done by the same artist or artists of the same period and style, and (b) choose five to ten works of diverse structural and expressive character, style, and subject which are reproduced in this text (or any set of reproductions of works of art that are readily accessible to each student for study.) After the student has carefully analyzed each work, he should compare and judge them, and record his judgments, in order of preference. He will hand in one copy of his judgments to the teacher and keep one for himself.

This, then, is to be followed by a discussion period, to be carried out in the same fashion as noted in the above section. Again, list any changes or enrichment of judgments.

PHASE IV Essay Assignment:

It may prove fruitful for each student to review in writing all the suggestions presented in class, including his own, as to what makes a good work of art or a bad work, giving examples. The student should compose an essay listing and discussing fully the reasons that he considers important in making judgments. Also consideration should be made as to what the student considers to be unimportant reasons or factors in judging works of art. A group discussion may follow.

These exercises have been designed so that the student can gain a wider base of experience for his judgments in a relatively small time; and if the exercises in judgment are diligently carried out, the students will have realized an increase in skill of judgment.

EXERCISE IN CREATING WORKS OF ART

It is now appropriate to present a carefully planned sequence of exercises to stimulate the individual's potential artistic ability in organizing the visual and expressive qualities into a creative work of art. Each exercise involves a basically different approach where certain conditions must be fulfilled, and brings in to play different means and factors in establishing unity within variety, balance and hierarchy. Theoretically, an infinite number of artistic solutions in a variety of styles are possible in each exercise.

The four basic exercises are divided into two main sections. In the first part (A) the works are to be symmetrically balanced. In the second part (B) the works should be asymmetrically balanced. It is suggested that the works should first be done with abstract forms; after which the exercises may be repeated employing the use of realistic elements. It is important to note that repeating the exercises may prove to steadily increase the effects of the student gaining practice in dealing with artistic solutions.

Each of the four basic exercises outlined below should be repeated twice. The artist's important task is to make each of the eight works as different as possible in the visual appearance and expression in accordance with the principles of art.

One should experiment with different methods in producing works of art. We list a few of the basic methods. One can begin by simply using a single visual element, for example, shape, to indicate the linear aspects of the work. This acts as a foundation upon which to develop the brightness and color aspects of the work. This can also lead to an alteration of the arrangement of shapes to more perfectly function within the new and more advanced stages of the development of the work.

We can observe some interesting evidence in a photomicrograph of a detail from C. Massys' panel (*Figure 154*) of the artist's changes made during the execution of the work. We observe above the small book in the man's hand the previous larger version of its shape which he drew before beginning to paint, which has struck through the paint layers over the centuries.

Another method is to begin by concentrating the greater part of one's attention on first establishing the visual and expressive character of the dominant form or patterns in the work. This is then followed by treating the visual and expressive properties to be introduced into the remaining sections of the work to suit or artistically unify the nature and character of the dominant form or pattern. The opposite of this method can be found in an unfinished panel by Albrecht Durer, "Salvator Mundi" (*Figure 155*), where the central form of the face is just linearly indicated with most of the remaining areas painted in quite carefully. The parallel situation is found in the analysis of the figure of Christ in Rembrandt's etching (*Figures 132-134*).

Another basic method is evident in some of the last unfinished works of Cezanne which have aesthetic completeness. The work was developed as a whole from the very beginning. Even if the artist's intention may change, but within this method the work is still conceived and developed in terms of its whole qualities.

Whatever methods are used, constant adjustments must be made during the creative process. For whenever a change is made it changes the visual and expressive identity of the work and therefore, there may be forms within the work that have to be modified or changed to fit in with the new state of the work. A work of art is never developed piecemeal in isolated stages. The artist's concept of the whole quality of the finished work is an important guiding factor in the development of the parts, sections or a single aspect of the work.

It is recommended that the artist begin with making several small preparatory studies for each exercise. It will be valuable that these studies be viewed by oneself and others as an insight into the genesis of each finished work.

After each work and the studies for them is completed they should be signed and numbered in the order they are done. A discussion can be carried out beginning with the individual describing his aims, experience gained and any difficulty felt. Then others present their analysis and judgment on two basic levels: (1) If the work fulfills the general requirements of artistic order; and (2) how well did the artist carry out his artistic intention. The major purpose of this classroom discussion is to present a wide range of views which parallels the purpose and points covered in the brainstorming and aesthetic judgment series.

Materials: It is suggested to use 9" x 12" or 12" x 18" paper. The standard set of tempera colors used in the previous exercises can be applied pure or intermixed to produce a wide range of colors.

Symmetrically Balanced Exercises

All the works done in this first part are to be symmetrically balanced. It is not recommended that the two halves be visually identical. The counterbalancing of the weights of the forms should be approximate with a variation in their

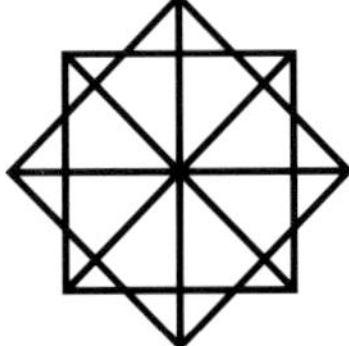
Figure 148

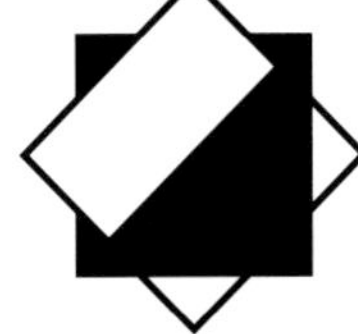
Figure 149

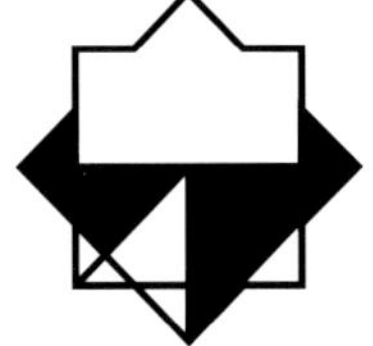
Figure 150

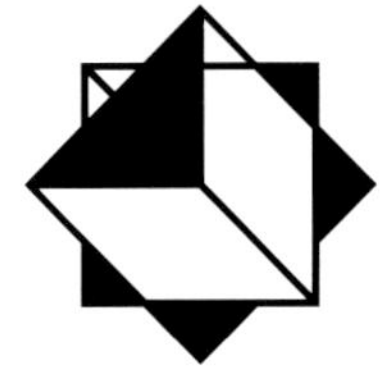
Figure 151

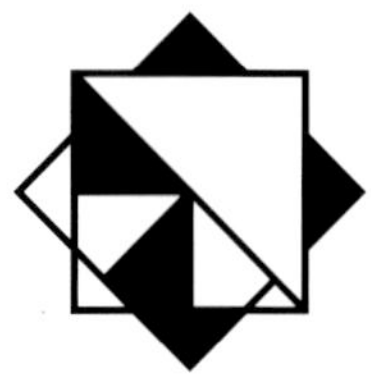
Figure 152

visual and expressive character. It is important to remember that only the dominant patterns need be symmetrically balanced while other aspects of the work need not be. We shall list below certain visual means which the individual is restricted to in each exercise as to how unity within variety and hierarchy is to be structurally achieved.

EXERCISE 1

(A) Unity within Variety: (1) Unify all the dominant patterns or forms in the work with a general similarity of brightness, and the remaining areas are to be somewhat similar in brightness to it. (Refer to Picasso's "Woman in White", *Figure 39*).

(2) To aid the unification of the different forms in the work use soft colors (blue and green with white and black). These colors can be used pure and intermixed (refer to pre-outlined exercises 18-24).

(3) In this exercise vary most of the visual properties of shape, such as the boundaries or structural orientation. (Refer to pp. 1-2 of the book). It may prove useful to review the text and exercises on unity within variety.

(B) Hierarchy: Let the dominant visual patterns or forms of the work complement or approximately complement the structural map with the subordinate patterns counterpointing it within the picture space. (Refer to Villon's "Abstraction" - *Figure 110*, and Braque's "The Cup" - *Figure 111*).

EXERCISE 2

(A) Unity within Variety: (1) Have the dominant patterns unified through similarity of shape properties. The subordinate patterns are to be unified through a degree of similarity of brightness.

(2) In addition to white and black, this exercise will require both hard (red and yellow) and soft (blue and green) colors; all of which can be used pure or intermixed.

(B) Hierarchy: Counterpoint the dominant pattern or patterns with the structural map with greater visual depth in the picture space used in exercise 1 (refer to Cezanne's "Bathers" - *Figure 118*). This will create a situation where the individual will begin to control the spatial intervals between the forms in the picture space (refer to page 48).

Asymmetrically Balanced Exercises

In this second part all the works are to be asymmetrically balanced. It may be useful to first review the text on asymmetrical balance and the experience gained from the previous exercises.

EXERCISE 3

(A) Unity within Variety: Use one or two of the visual elements (shape, brightness, and color) to contribute to unifying the dominant visual and expressive properties of the work. The remaining areas of the work should contribute to the attainment of variety. Use all the six standard colors pure or intermixed.

(B) Hierarchy: Let the dominant patterns counterpoint the structural map within the visual picture space.

EXERCISE 4

(A) Unity within variety: Let each of the visual elements (shape, brightness and color) contribute approximately equally to achieving unity within variety in the work.

(B) Hierarchy: In this final exercise let the pattern be in full visual counterpoint with each other and the structural map within the picture space, as in Rubens' "Wolf and Fox Hunt" (*Figure 103*).

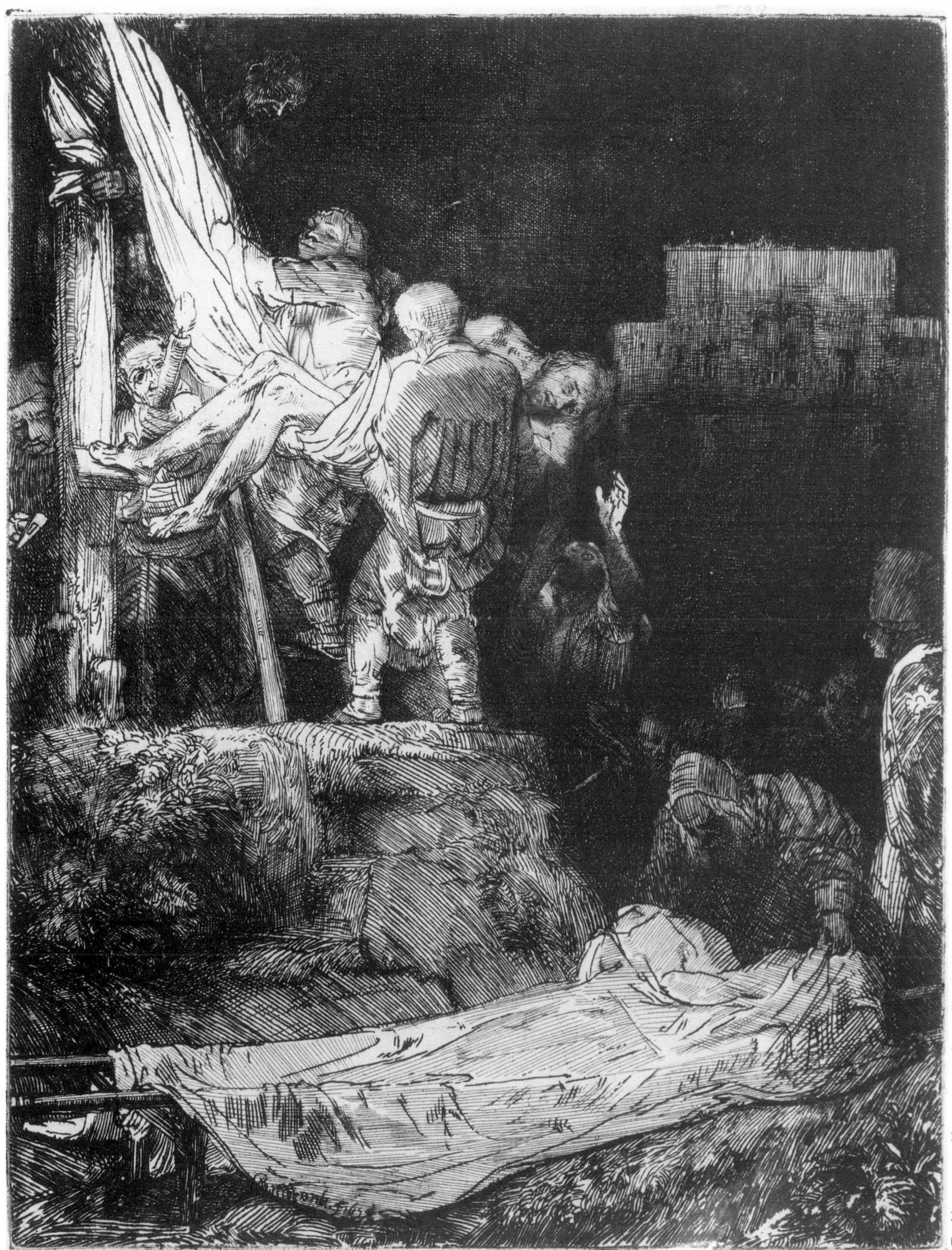

Figure 153. REMBRANDT, DESCENT FROM THE CROSS BY TORCHLIGHT

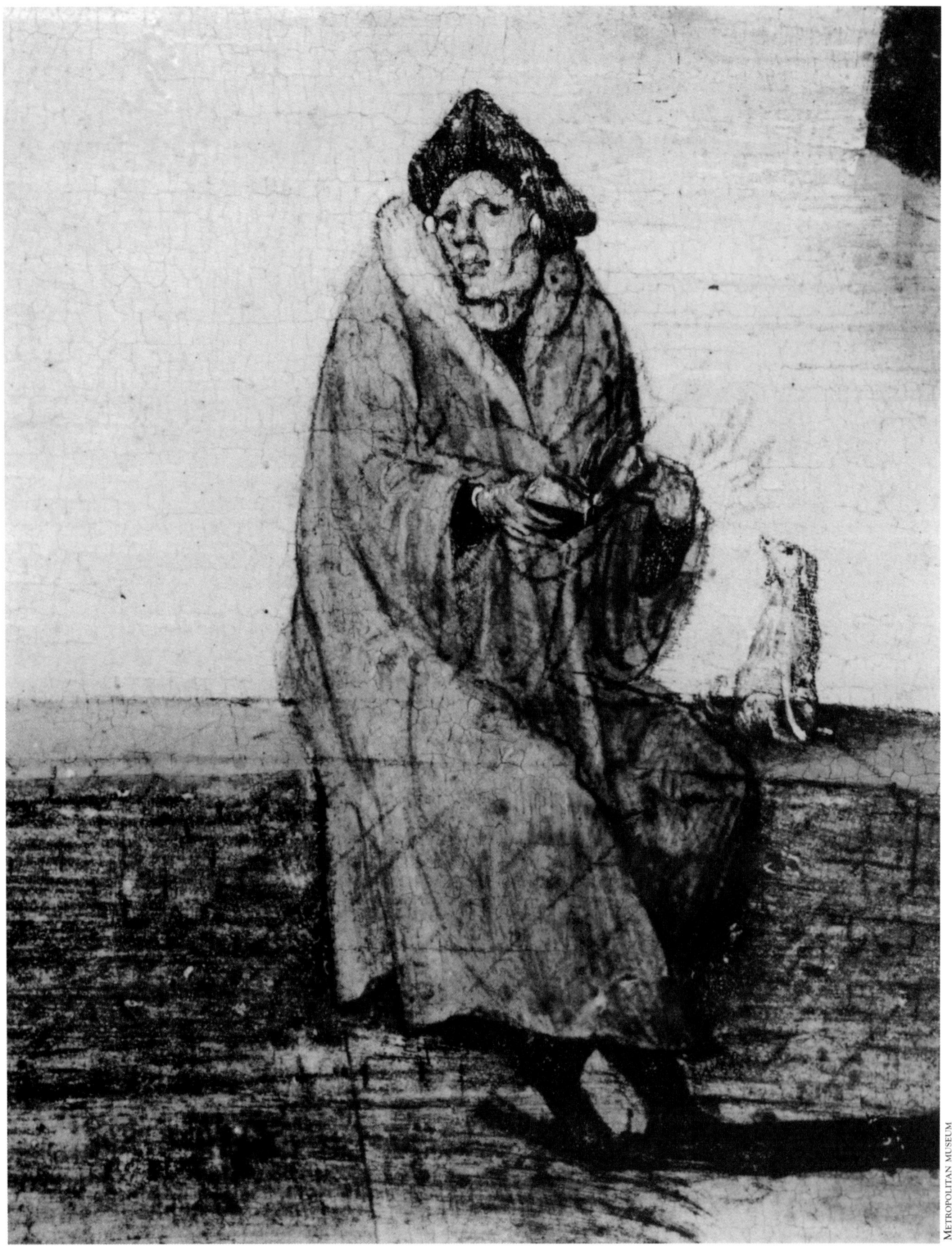

Figure 154. CORNELIS MASSYS, THE ARRIVAL IN BETHLEHEM (ENLARGED DETAIL)

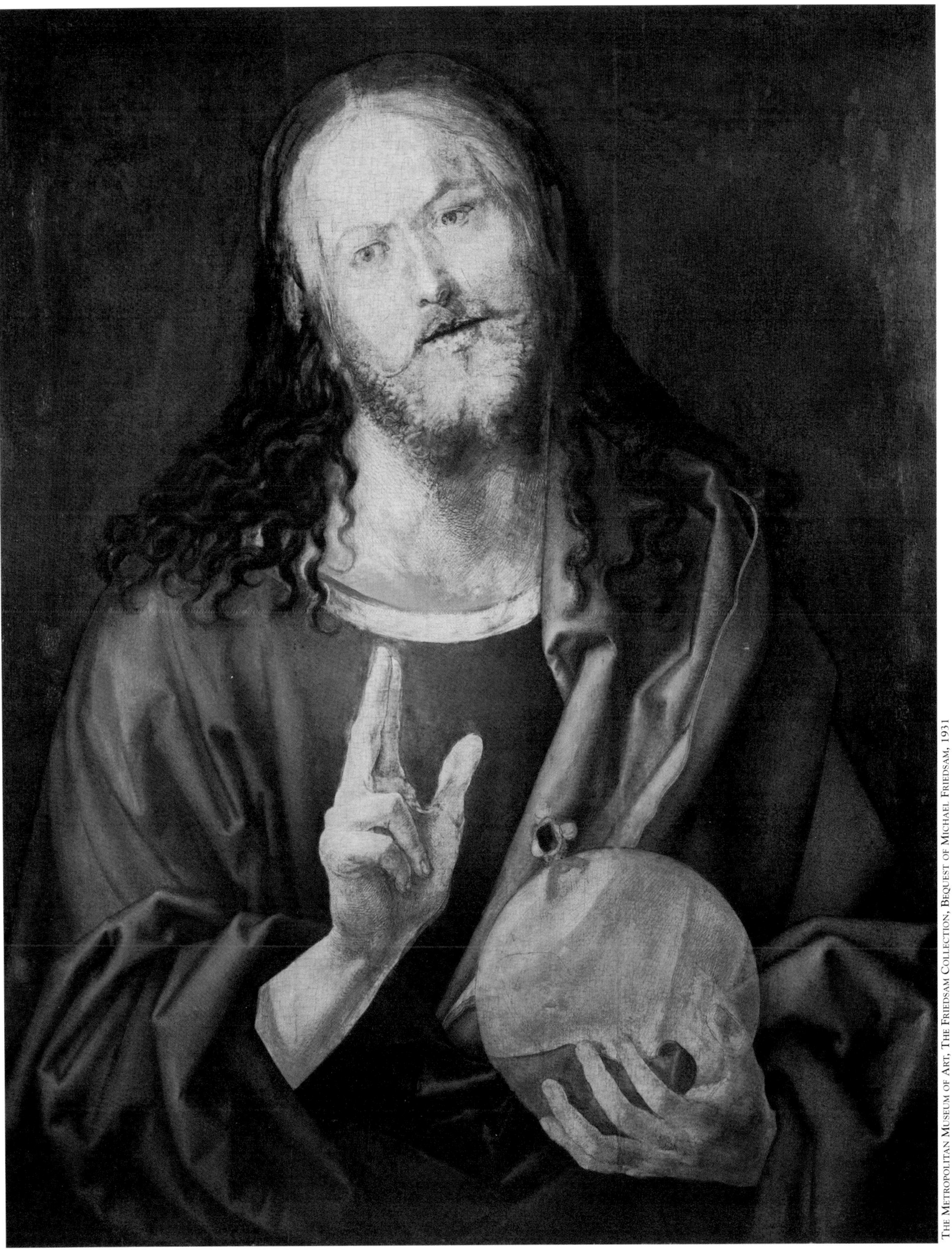

The Metropolitan Museum of Art, The Friedsam Collection, Bequest of Michael Friedsam, 1931

Figure 155. DURER, SALVATOR MUNDI

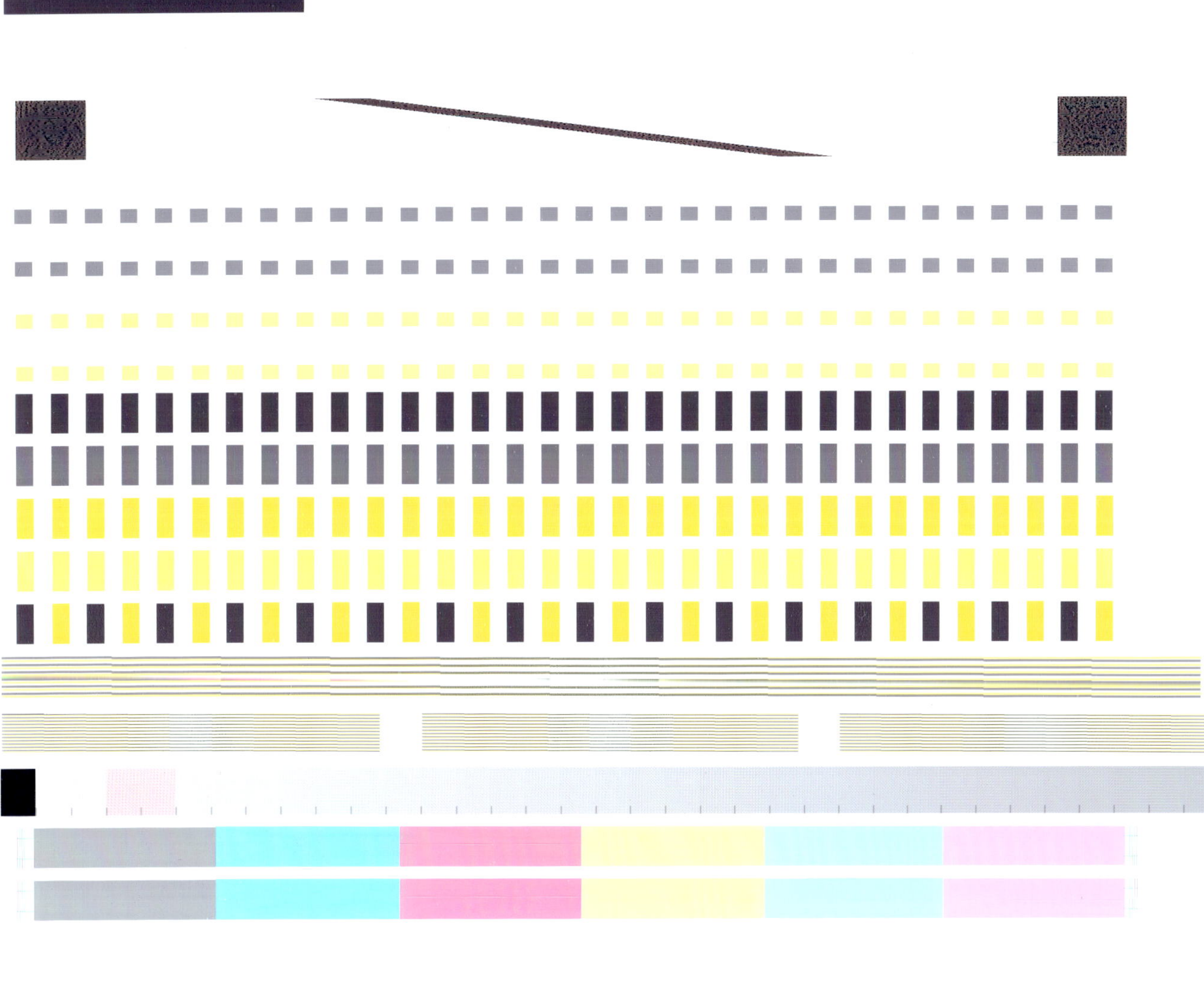

Pre-Outlined Exercise Sheet 1

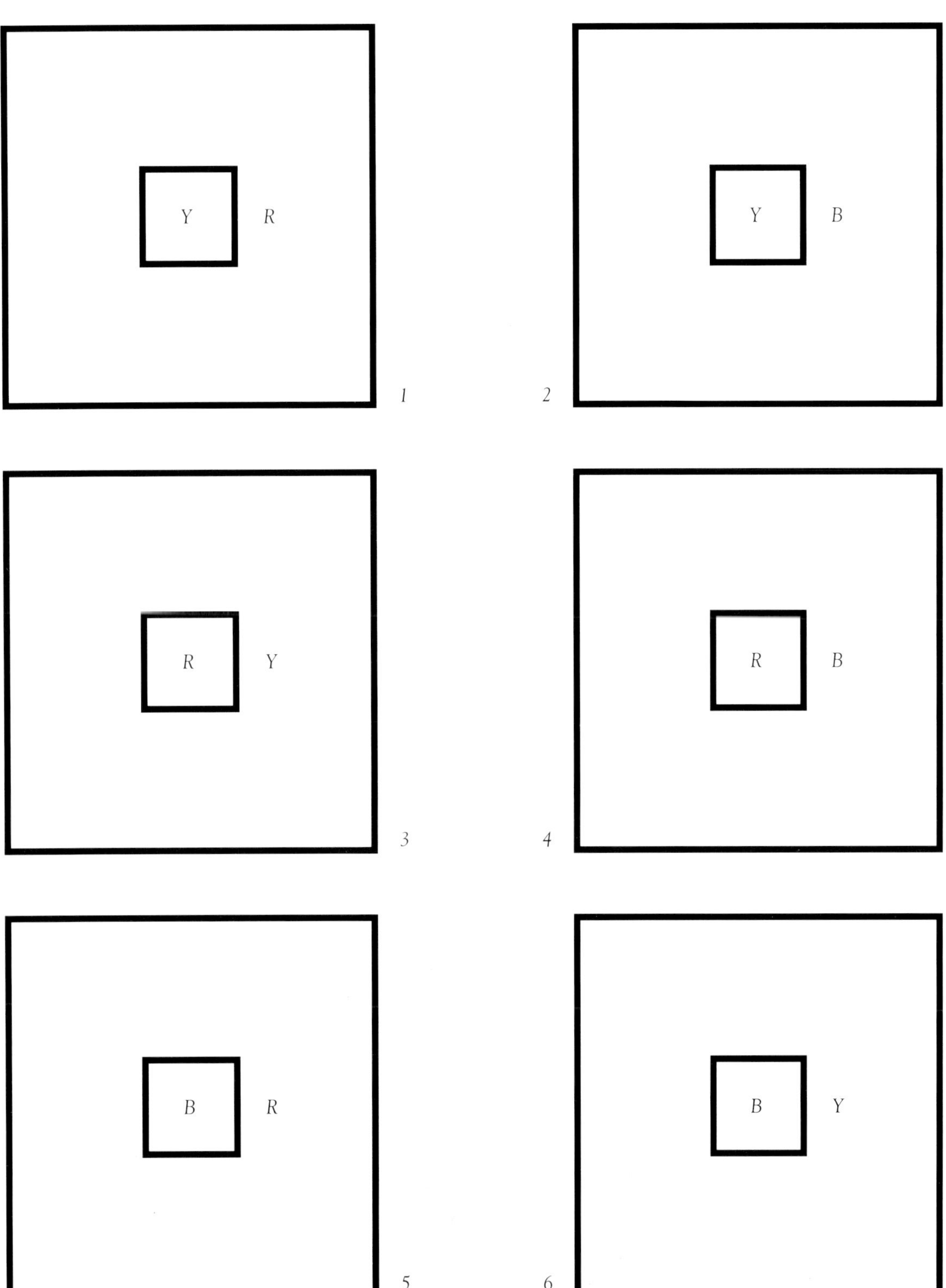

Pre-Outlined Exercise Sheet 2

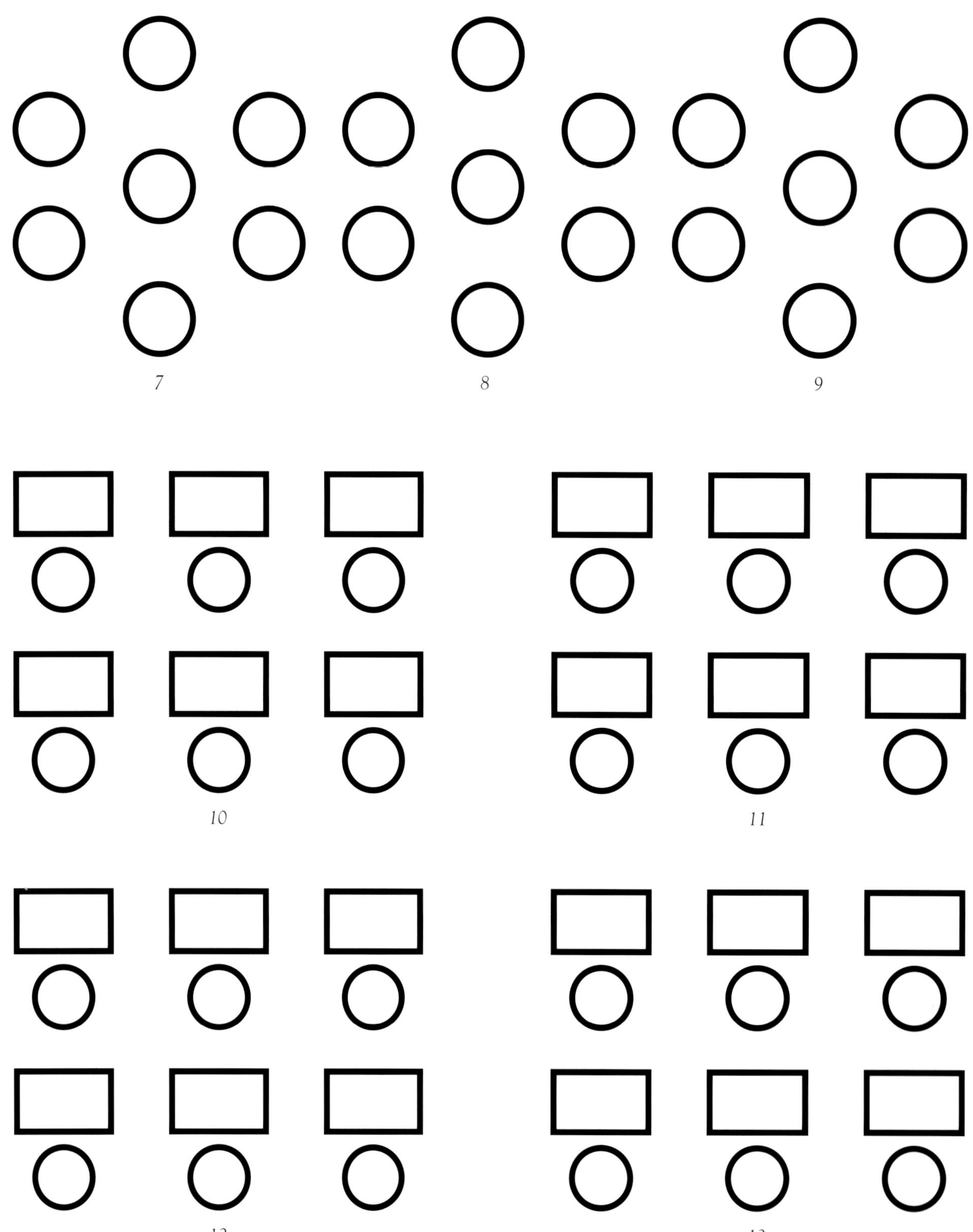

Pre-Outlined Exercise Sheet 3

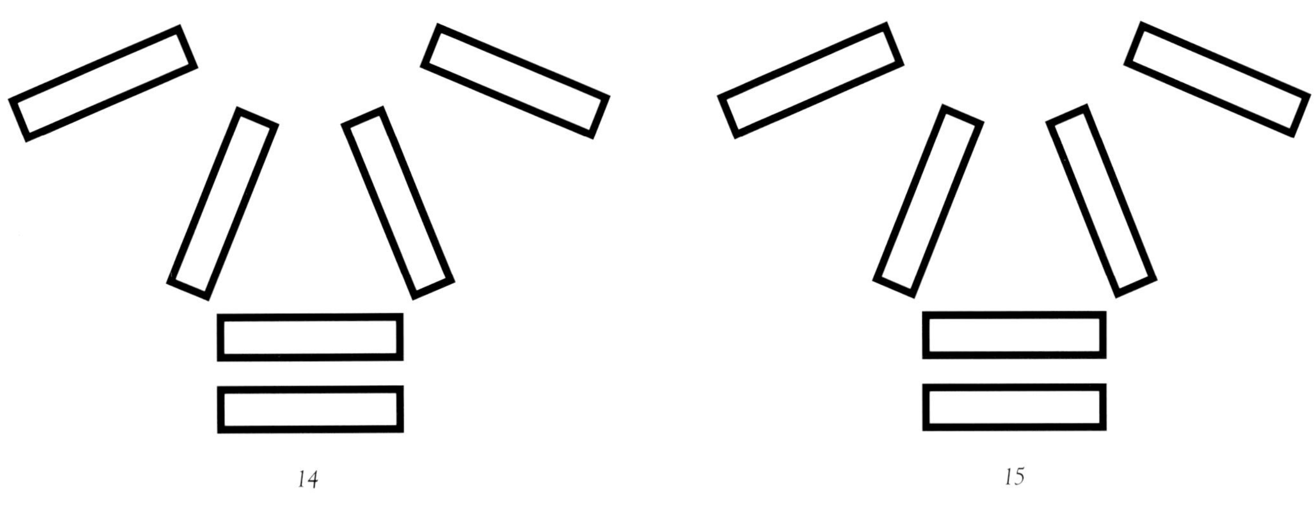

14 15

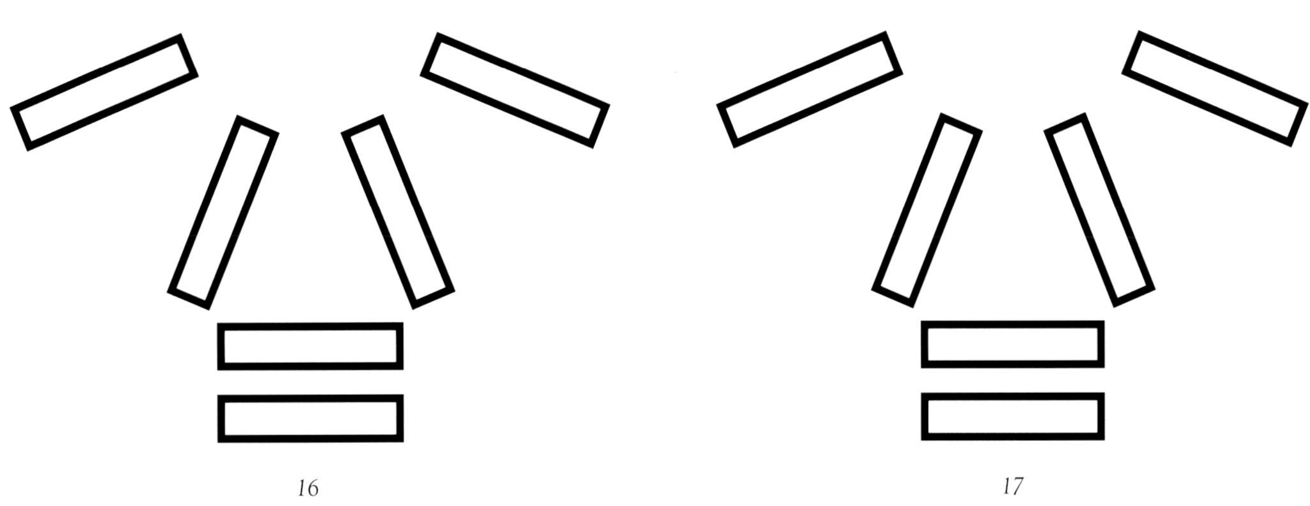

16 17

PRE-OUTLINED EXERCISE SHEET 4

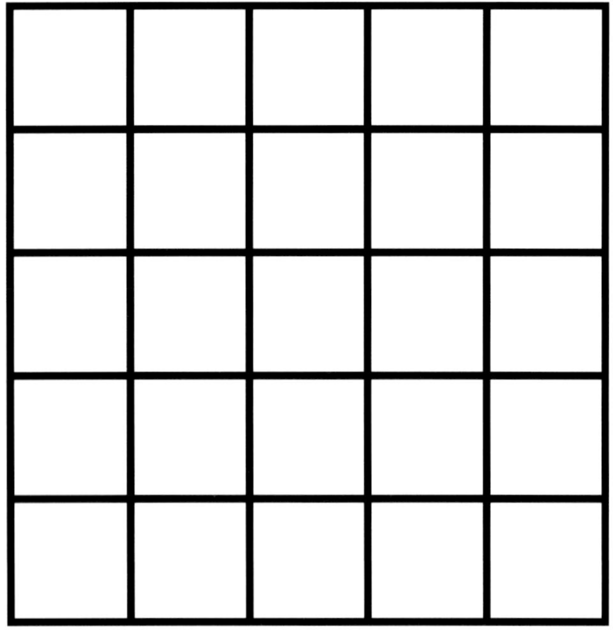

18

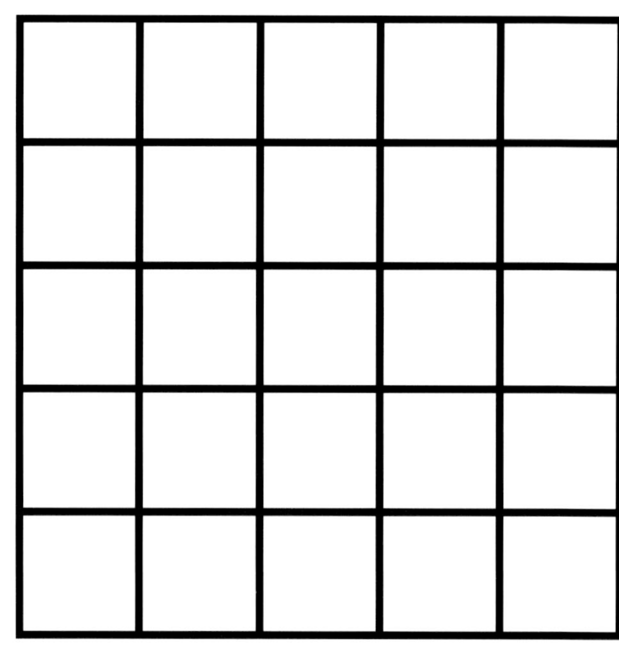

19

20

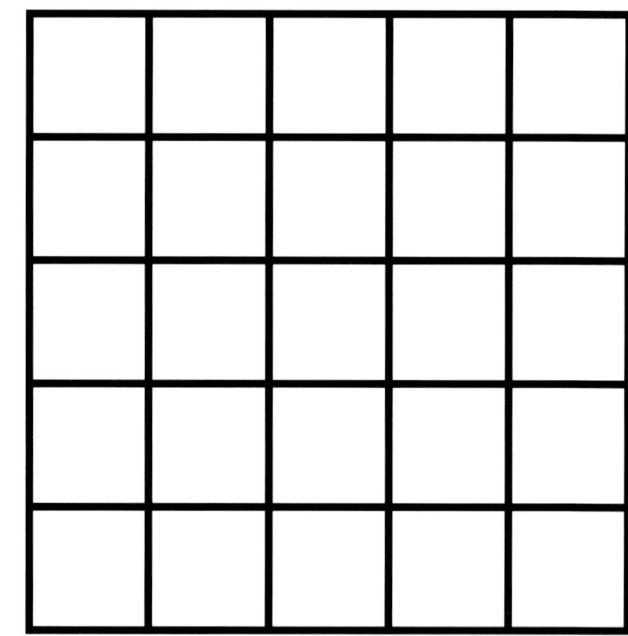

21

PRE-OUTLINED EXERCISE SHEET 5

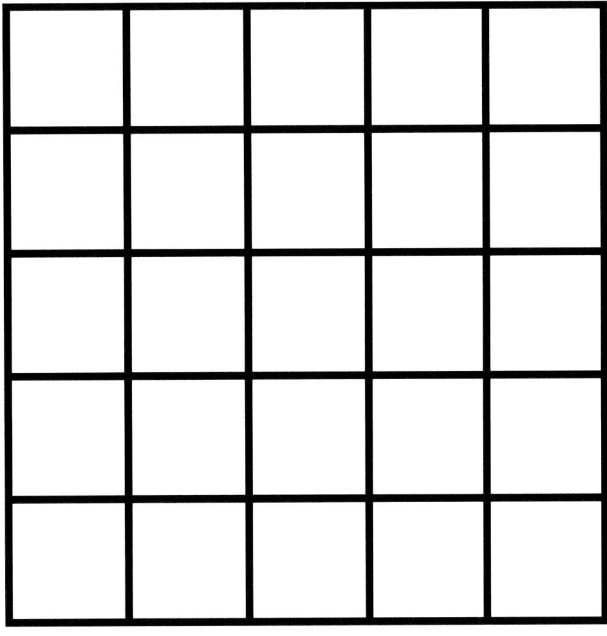

22

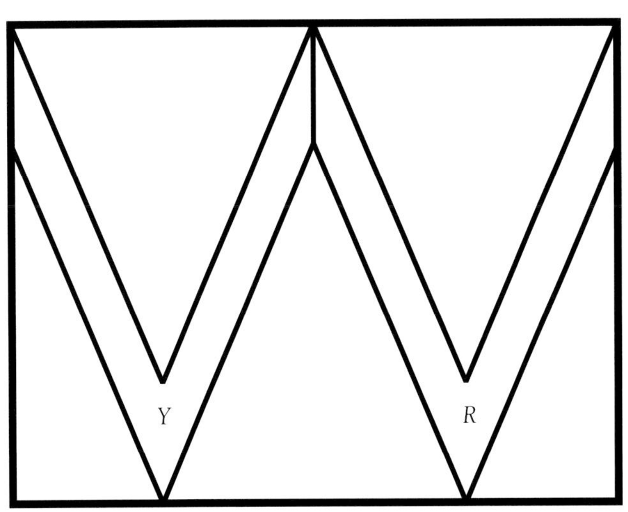

23

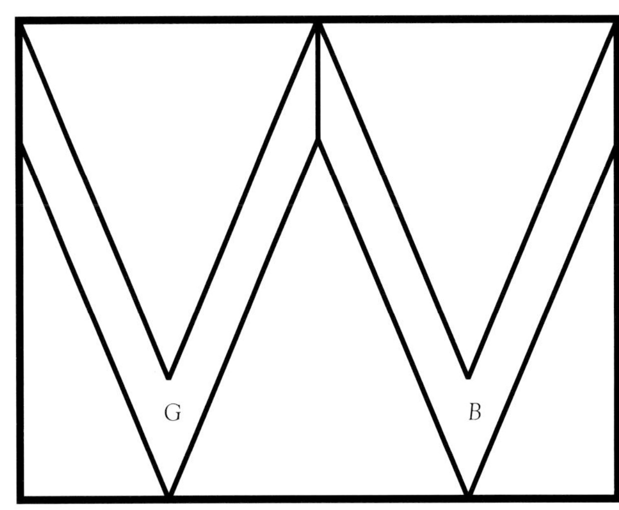

24

Pre-Outlined Exercise Sheet 6

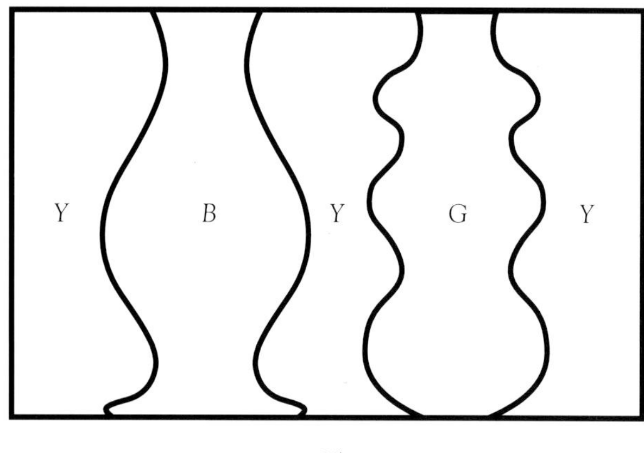

25

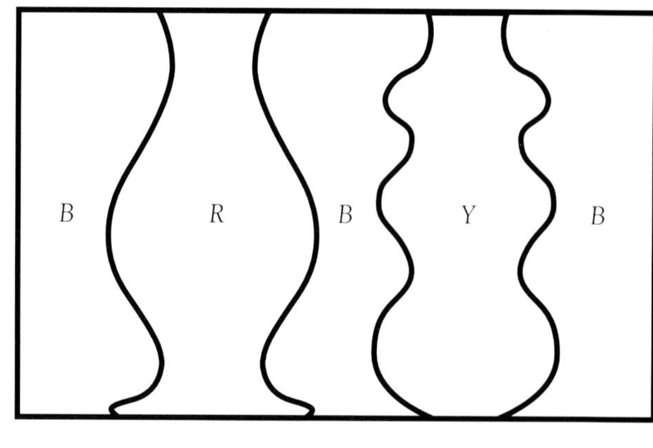

26

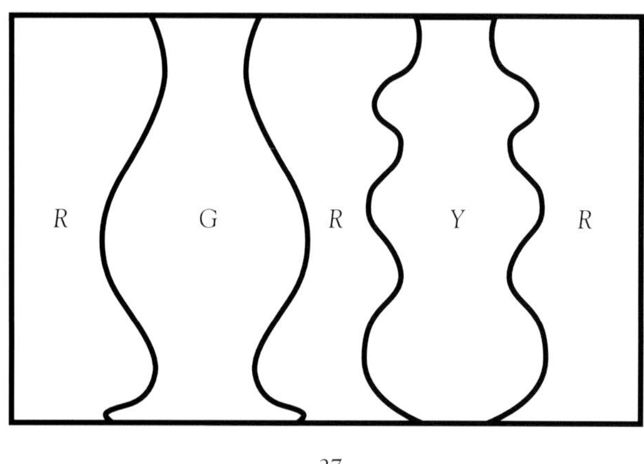

27

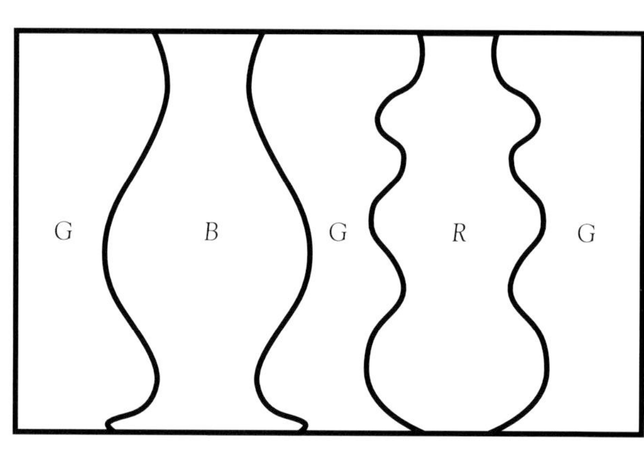

28

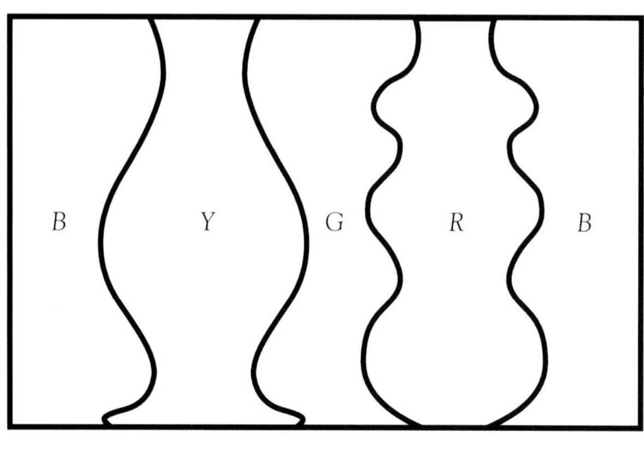

29

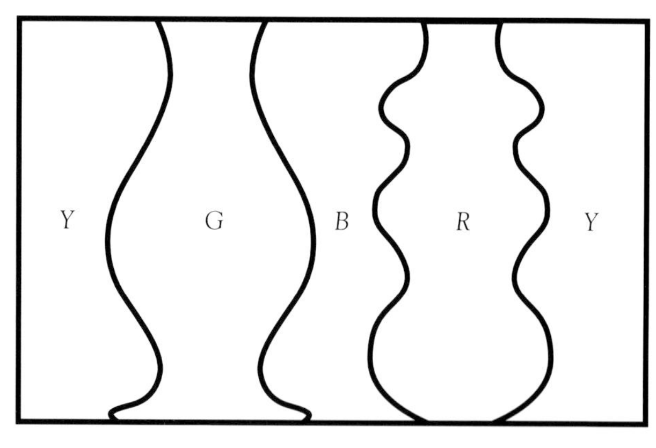

30

PRE-OUTLINED EXERCISE SHEET 7

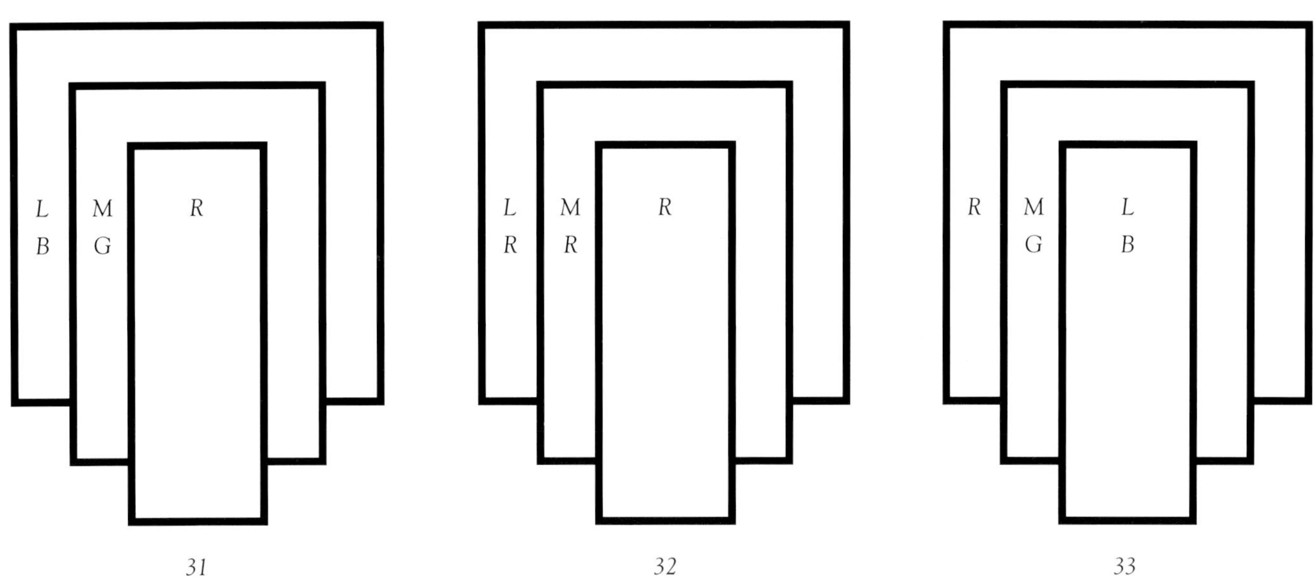

31 32 33

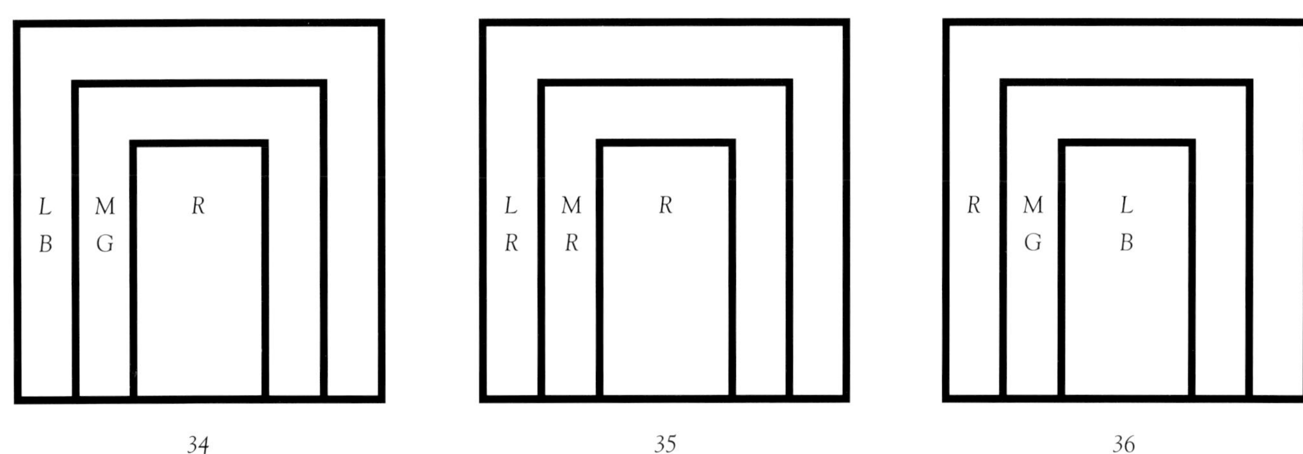

34 35 36

PRE-OUTLINED EXERCISE SHEET 8

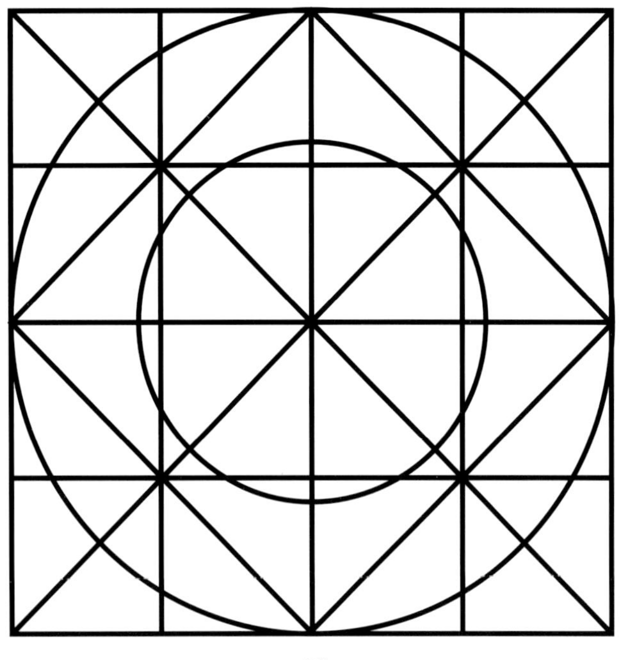

37

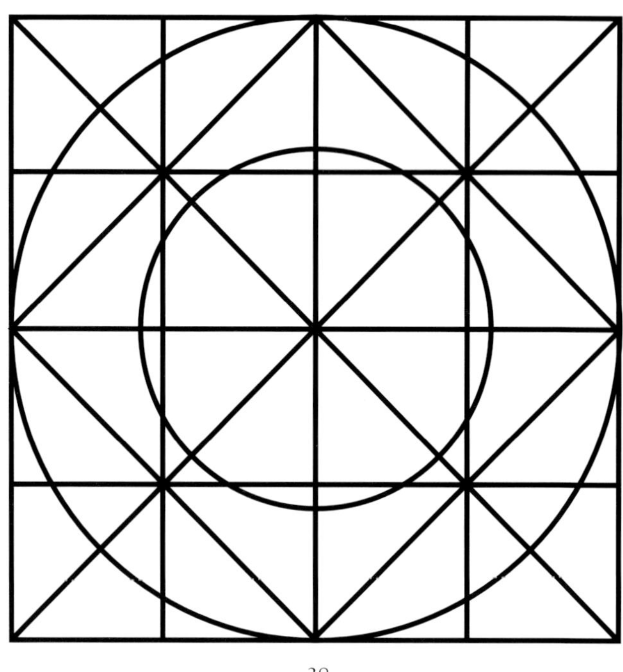

38

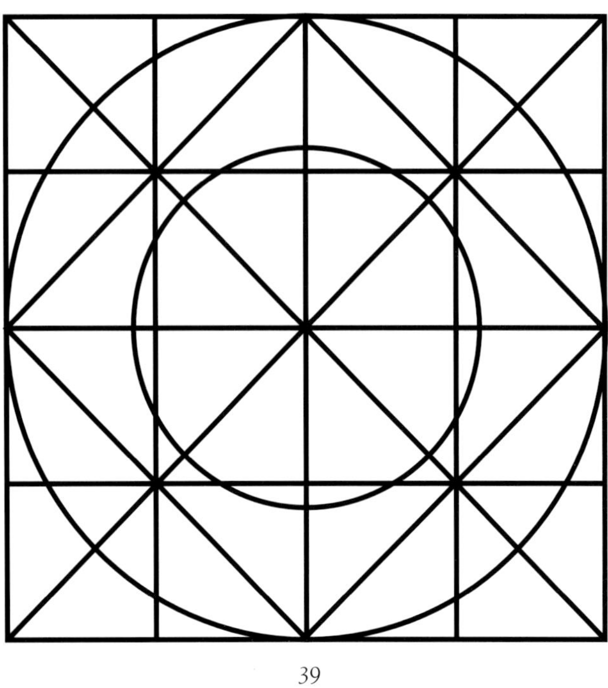

39

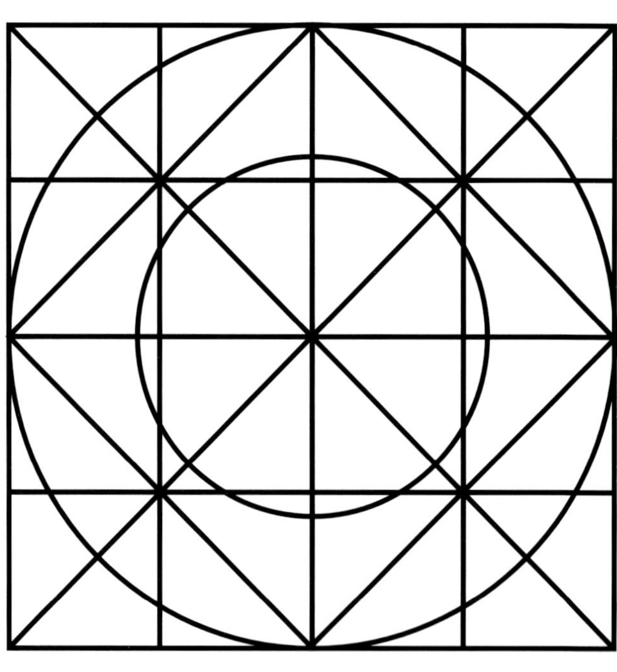

40

Pre-Outlined Exercise Sheet 10

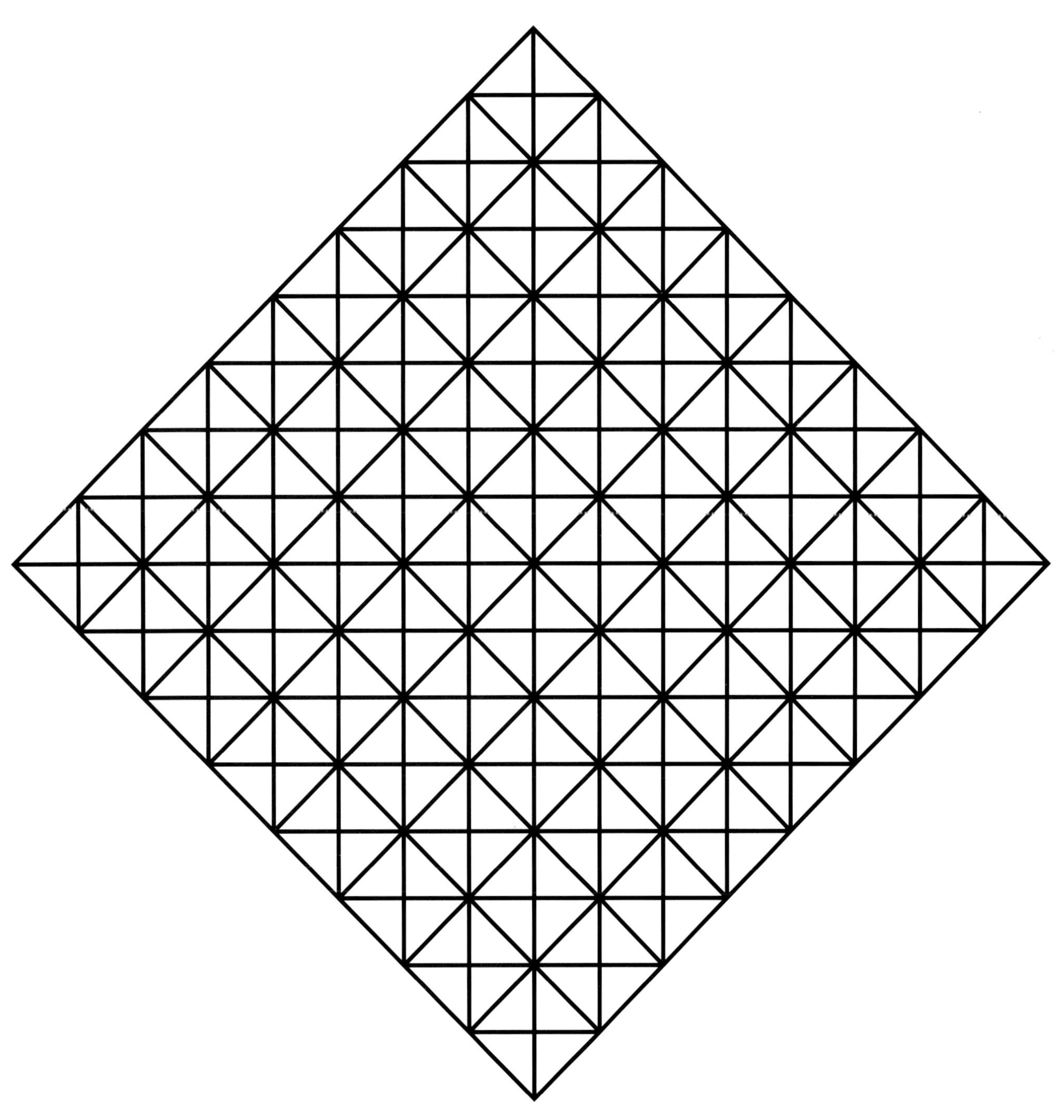

42

Pre-Outlined Exercise Sheet 9

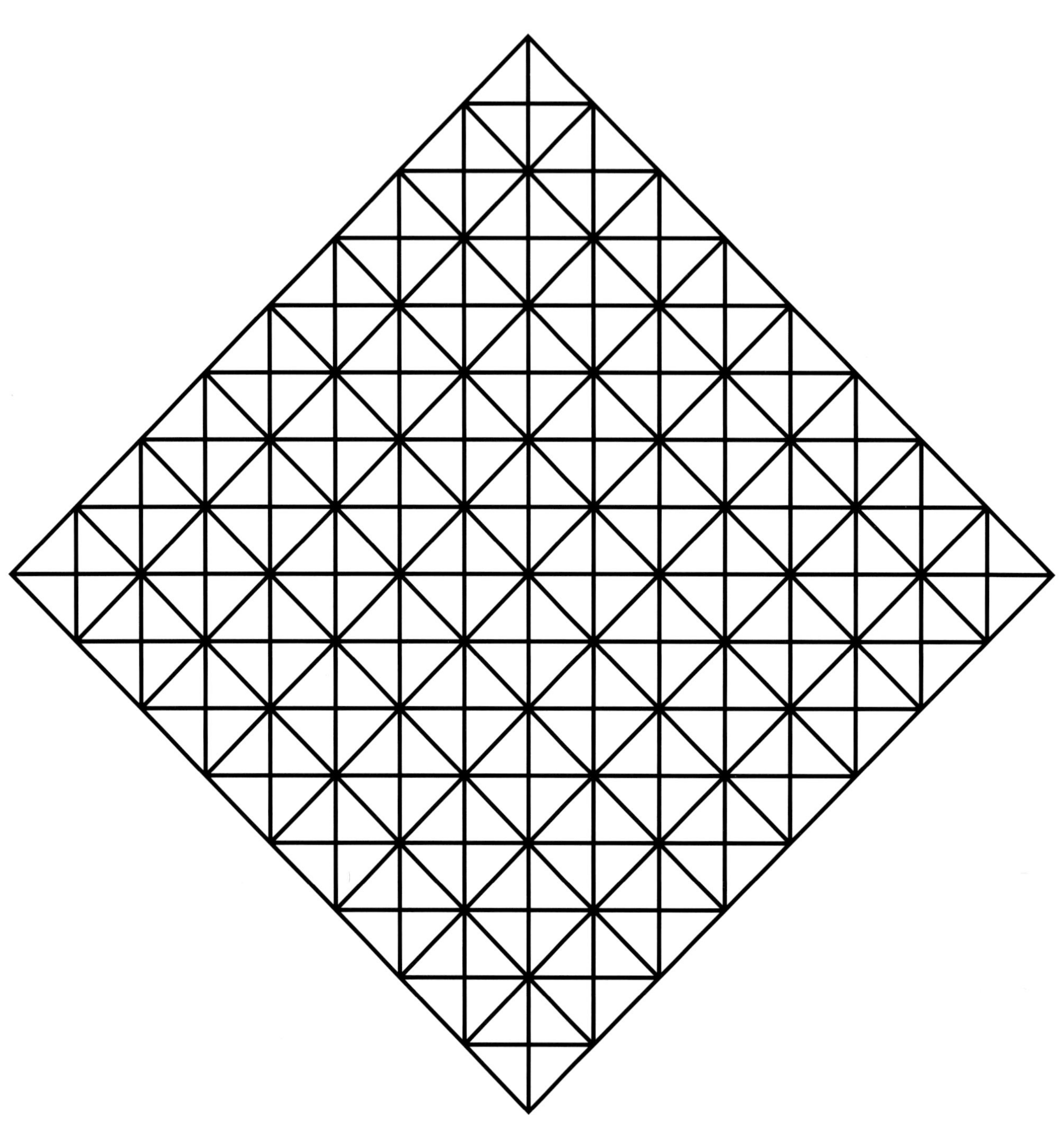

41